Our Lady
of Licheń

The Sorrowful Queen of Poland
awaits you in Her sanctuary at Licheń

Father Eugeniusz Makulski

On the 30th Anniversary of the Pontifical Coronation of the
Holy Image of Our Lady of Licheń

*This booklet is dedicated to the praise of Mary, and to the joy
and encouragement of those who honour Her.*

Father Eugeniusz Makulski, MIC

Licheń, 1967-1997

© Wydawnictwo ZET® Wrocław 2001
Text by Father Eugeniusz Makulski
Photographs by Romuald M. Sołdek, Tomasz Szarski, Edmund Wojnarowski
L'Osservatore Romano — Servizio Fotografico
Translated by Teresa Bałuk-Ulewiczowa
Graphics by Małgorzata Bełdowska
All rights reserved
tel.: (071) 332 37 47; (071) 783 28 64
fax: (071) 332 39 93
e-mail: wydawnictwozet@foxnet.pl
ISBN: 83-88759-00-0

TO THOSE HEARTS IN WHICH POLISH BLOOD FLOWS...

O, beloved Mother of God, O, Mary, Sorrowful Queen of Poland, I humbly beseech You to grant many graces and blessings, and especially the Gifts of the Holy Spirit to the one who has now taken up this booklet which tells the story of Your great mercy on the Polish Nation and on each and every human being without exception.

O, Mary, to You I commend the body and soul, the life and health of that person. Dearest Mother, be near while this booklet is being read and envelop in Your maternal love one more — perhaps deeply suffering and lost — human soul.

Each time I kneel before the Miraculous Image of Our Lady of Licheń, I always pray for those who read these pages, for their souls to open to a joyous experience and for them as if personally to encounter the Blessed Virgin.

Today I commend you, my dear friend, to the love of our Heavenly Mother and Queen of the Polish Nation. I do not ask who you are or what your profession is, or of your opinions. I do not ask about your life — whether it has been saintly or sinful — or what the present state of your soul is. It matters not whether you have just started out on life in this world and are full of energy, or whether perhaps your life is behind you already and you are standing, full of uncertainty, before the gates of eternity. If these words have reached you today, I am sure Mary has looked graciously upon you, that She wishes to bestow graces on you, that She wishes to speak to you, that She has some secret intentions with respect to you. So take this book and read it!

In 1850 the Mother of God came down from Heaven as the Queen of Poland, bringing an admonition and consolation for the Polish Nation, which was then suffering in the bonds of enthralment, and for all distressed human souls.

In modern Poland there are 430 places of pilgrimage with shrines of Our Lady

What you are about to read here is for you and others, for the Holy Virgin's message has always been addressed to those hearts in which there in Polish blood, wherever they may be in the world. Now the Blessed Mother of God wishes these words to reach you, through them She wants to manifest Herself to you. She wishes to make known to you Her care and Her maternal love. She would like you to be Her messenger. So do not reject this letter. Do not turn down this calling; find a quiet spot and some free time to read it carefully, opening up your heart and mind to the sweet voice of Mary. Submit to the divine inspiration of the Holy Spirit, and you will attain a profound experience, perhaps also to those graces you have been yearning for so long.

Our country's enemies have tried to do everything to prevent people from finding out about Our Lady's apparitions at Licheń, Poland's Lourdes. What the foreign partitioning powers found

Our Lady's face from the Holy Image of Licheń

→

most unbearable was the fact that the Virgin Mary would appear with the Polish White Eagle on her heart, that She forecast the restoration of Poland, that She promised Her spiritual assistance, and that She confirmed the Nation's flagging spirit.

The Partitioners persecuted and imprisoned the herdsman Mikołaj; they suppressed articles in the press and information in books on the apparitions. Priests were forbidden to mention Licheń in sermons. Difficulties were created for pilgrims making their way to this holy place. There was even a time when attempts were made to confiscate and destroy the miraculous picture of the Sorrowful Virgin of Licheń.

But Our Lady did not permit the total frustration of Her will; She did not allow the new sanctuary She had founded to be brought down. A variety of difficulties, especially the lack of publications, have made Our Lady's meaningful and beautiful apparitions at Licheń less well known than they deserve to be. First Poland's lack of independence at the time, then the First World War followed by two hard decades between the Wars, and the Nazi occupation of Poland during the Second World War, were responsible for the inadequate level of development and organisation of this shrine.

In other countries where there have been apparitions of Our Lady today there are splendid churches, chapels, basilicas, pilgrims' houses and monasteries. There are good roads to these places. The bishops and priests talk about the apparitions in their sermons, and they encourage people to make pilgrimages to such places. Pilgrims travel hundreds of miles, just to visit a shrine where the Virgin Mary has appeared at least once in their lives. They go there to pray and to be strengthened spiritually.

Here at Licheń it's different. In Grąblin Wood, where Our Lady walked and appeared to Mikołaj, there is a tiny chapel with what remains of the historic pine-tree.

On Licheń Hill, the place where the Miraculous Picture is situated, only a small, low church with a straw-lined ceiling next to an equally exiguous presbytery, a hundred and thirty years old, was built in the first century following the apparitions. Moreover even this tiny church was devastated during the Second World War.

Unfortunately, this is all that could be done to thank the Lord for the miracle of Our Lady's apparitions and for the innumerable graces which have come and continue to come from this holy hill for the entire Nation. Licheń is an excellent example illustrating the old Polish proverb, "Ye praise the foreign, but fail to know what ye have at home."

We have many magnificent shrines of Our Lady in Poland. They have been raised over the centuries by kings, princes, lords, rich monasteries and millions of generous men and women. But we do not have so many places which Mary chose for Herself and where She appeared, or paths on which She walked.

Licheń is one such spot, chosen by the Blessed Virgin Mary Herself, a place where She left vestiges of her footsteps.

We in Poland also have many magnificent images of the Blessed Mother. They are renowned for their graces and miracles; grateful hearts have showered a multitude of votive offerings of gold, silver, and diamonds on them. But there are few images which Our Lady Herself has discovered and touched during an apparition. The Miraculous Picture of Our Lady of Licheń is just such an image. It was discovered by Our Lady in the forest; She touched it with Her holy hand; She gave it to the Nation as a token of Her love and Her presence. She promised many graces to those who ask Her for grace before this image. She wants to be honoured in this image as the Mother and Sorrowful Queen of Poland.

She came down from Heaven not just to appear once to a cow-herd and leave him Her image, but spiritually She has stayed with us ever since.

Every pilgrim who comes to Licheń Church with a pure heart feels the living presence here of the Mother of God. She is here all the time, showering innumerable graces and miracles upon Her children.

The Virgin Mary has done everything to show that She is the most loving of mothers and the most gracious of queens. Now it is up to us to accord Her veneration and to fulfil Her wish for as many as possible of those who believe to learn of Her and to benefit by the graces flowing from this fount.

You are learning of this now; but try to make your family, your friends and acquaintances know about Licheń and learn how much Our Lady loves them. For over a thousand years the Virgin Mother of God has been the most loving of Mothers to the people of Poland; She has been our unfailing helper. Today She will help us free ourselves of our vices, our sins, and our weaknesses; She will help us in our spiritual and moral renewal. Mary will make us a nation of staunch faith, sobriety, and purity; She will bring about our happiness. There is no other way, no other rescue for us weak humans, except in the arms of Mary our Queen.

The following story is grounded on the results of the scholarship and research work which I have been conducting for several years now in my capacity as custodian of the shrine. The facts are documented in manuscripts and printed materials which were compiled immediately following the Licheń apparitions. There is also a number of extant official documents, which I have referred to.

The local folk tradition, which is extremely vigorous in the Parish of Licheń and its environs, has been an important source of information. The words Our Lady spoke, as well as Her prophecies have circulated widely among the people. But it has proved very difficult to establish some of these facts, due to the lack of source-materials, which probably existed once, but were lost during the War. Recently a large scholarly monograph was published about Licheń. It was translated into Latin and sent to the Holy See, with a petition for the coronation of the Miraculous Image. In this booklet the story will be quite brief, without the historical sources, since it is in fact a summary of the large book which contains all the most important items of information.

*P*icturesque view of the Shrine of Lichen from beyond the lake

———————➤

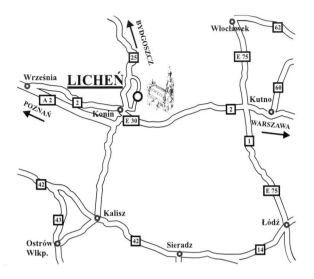

R*oad plan of the Licheń area*

As regards the apparitions themselves, their description has been deliberately limited to a brief account of three instances, although there were many apparitions. But I do not describe them because I do not have the full data available. Maybe one day someone will find better sources.

Our Lady's words are quoted partly after printed sources which came out directly after the apparitions themselves, and partly from the folk tradition, which I have endeavoured to examine in the neighbourhood of Licheń and the region around Konin. I would like to stress that the account of the apparitions complies with the facts; however the words used to express them have been adapted somewhat, since both the cowherd and the people of Licheń used their own local peasant dialect.

THE LEGEND AND HISTORY OF LICHEŃ

The village of Licheń Stary lies 10 kilometres north of the municipal boundary of Konin. At the crossroads before the hospital at Konin we take the road for Sompolno. We pass Morzysław Church and the bridge over the Warta and Gopło Canal, Laskówiec, and then we turn left. The asphalt road meanders among the fields, meadows, and dark forests past the villages of Wola Padłężna, Izabelin, and Grąblin. At the end of the Grąbliński Forest on the horizon we can see the village of Licheń straddled out along the lakeside, and the monastery buildings of the shrine. Just beyond the lake there is a hill surmounted by a church up to which a path with wide steps leads. From the church-tower there is a panorama view to be had over the entire, beautiful countryside of Konin. The area is slightly undulating, and you can see numerous patches of woodland, the silver mirrors of several lakes, arable fields, broad meadows in the ancient valley of the River Warta, many villages and church-towers. To the west are the outlines of the slag-tips of the area's huge coal mines, and the perpendicular chimneys of the electricity power station and several other industrial plants. To the south are the housing estates and high-rise tower blocks of Konin new town.

Licheń itself is a quiet settlement amid the lakes, woodland, and meadows. The grounds of the shrine are quite large, afforested and full of flowers and extend over the hill within a high perimeter wall. Inside this enclosure there are sites where religious services are celebrated: an outdoor way of the Cross, a path with the mysteries of the rosary, outdoor altars, chapels, crosses and holy statues, monuments, historic tombs, figures of the saints, quiet footpaths and havens of peace. There is also the Church of Our Lady of Częstochowa, which was built in 1971, along with the Holy Cross Chapel and a graveyard beyond it. In the middle stands the brick-built Church of St. Dorothy, which houses the Miraculous Image of Our Lady. Everywhere here there are excellent conditions for prayer, retreats, and contemplation: an opportunity for the soul to encounter God and to talk to Mary.

The place has an ancient history. It was inhabited as long ago as the Stone Age; a variety of Neolithic tools in stone and flint have been excavated on the hill. In Roman times a trading route known as the Amber Way passed through this region. Legend has it that there was a pagan temple among the ancient trees on the hill, and that Satan, the Prince of Darkness, was worshipped there. The Slavonic word "licho," from which the place-name Licheń is derived, means "the evil one." People from the entire neighbourhood came here to worship the granite idol, offer up sacrifices to it, and cast spells and practise their superstitions.

In 1969 mysterious stone blocks and rocks were unearthed here. They probably came from the dismantled pagan altar, and the stones used for the performance of the pagan rites. When God called the Polish people to the true faith, when the light of the Gospels came to Poland, the pagan temple here was demolished and a cross was fashioned out of the granite idol. Since 1151 this cross has stood on the green in the middle of the village. Invaders submerged this cross in the lake, but once the war was over, it was retrieved and put up in its old place.

In the 13th century a castle owned by the noble and famous family of Licheński stood at the crest of the hill, surrounded by a thriving and populous town. A series of well-known historical figures, voivodes, bishops, knights, and even the Chancellor of the Realm in the days of Queen Jadwiga and King Jagiełło (late 14th century) was born in this castle. Another historic personality born in Licheń was Andrzej Licheński, later Bishop of Poznań and one of the creators of the Union of Poland and Lithuania.

The town was destroyed in 1655 during the Swedish Invasion. The Swedes besieged and soon captured Licheń; they looted and destroyed its two churches, castle, and the town itself. They rounded up all of its inhabitants, from infants to old men, on the lakeside and on the port-bridges, and massacred them. The water in the lake was red with human blood.

Only a handful of the local people — soldiers and those who managed to hide in the forests and marshes around the Warta before the siege started — survived the Swedish War. Licheń never returned to its former status, and its lost its municipal rights. Today it owes its reputation to the fact that Our Lady chose this charming part of Poland for Her special place of veneration.

LOST HOPES

On 20th October 1813 the War of the Nations drew to a close on the battlefield of Leipzig in Saxony. 130 thousand died in the four days of this mortal conflict involving nearly half a million soldiers from all the countries of Europe.

The great Napoleon, "War-God" and Emperor of France, Poland's last hope for the retrieval of her independence forfeited ultimately in 1795, was lost in this battle when Napoleon was vanquished. The defeat of the French and Polish troops brought about not only the fall of the French Empire, but also what is sometimes referred to as the Fourth Partition of Poland. The Poles had expected Napoleon to subdue Russia, Prussia, and Austria, the three powers which had partitioned Poland, and thereby to obtain freedom and national union for Poland.

Over 10 thousand Polish soldiers, along with their supreme commander, Prince Józef Poniatowski, sacrificed their lives for Poland on the field at Leipzig. At the Congress of Vienna, where a new European order was established, none of the nations meeting "in concert" spoke up for Poland.

The Partitioners erased Poland off the maps of the world, condemning the wretched nation which all had forsaken to non-existence. But the people of Poland could not learn to live with the slavery into which they had been cast. Time and again uprisings would break down, which were brutally suppressed. Rivers of blood and tears soaked into the miserable land. The

Partitioners' prisons, dungeons and keeps filled up with the best sons of the Polish Nation.

For a hundred years no star of hope shone on the sombre Polish horizon except for one: Mary, the Mother of God. That Star never faded over the persecuted nation. The people would come to Her sanctuaries; they would voice their complaints to Her; and She would confirm them in their faith and put hope into failing hearts of better times, of freedom. The nation had neither a government of its own, nor an army of its own, nor an educational system. It only had its faith and the Mother of God, Who never forsook it and has ever remained on Her throne as Queen of Poland.

A SOLDIER'S LOT

The stately mansion set in extensive grounds and large country estate of fertile Cuiavian farmland near Izbica Kujawska belonged to Tomasz Kłossowski. He was a good master to his servants, generous to his country, and valorous in its defence. He participated in the wars and uprisings raised against the Partitioning powers, and for this he was punished severely. His property was confiscated and he was threatened with imprisonment. Dressed in peasants' clothing, he reached Izabelin in the Parish of Licheń, bought a small farm of 4 acres with a small house on it, next to which he set up a blacksmith's shop. Here he made farming tools for the peasants, and perhaps also war weapons; he put horseshoes on the peasants' draught-animals, but perhaps also on the insurgents' chargers? Soon another war broke out, so Tomasz closed down his smithy and set out to fight for Poland. He crossed half of Europe; he tasted the soldier's bitter lot; at Leipzig he fought to the last bullet. He was a witness to Prince Józef Poniatowski's heroic death; then enemy gunfire ripped through his right leg, side, and left him with a head injury.

Tomasz was near to death on account of these wounds and his total exhaustion. With the last of his strength he dragged himself into a nearby clump of bushes and awaiting his end started piously to call on the assistance of the Virgin Mary.

Great sorrow and longing for his country filled his soldier's heart. He did not want to die among strangers, on German soil, so he took out the medal of Our Lady of Częstochowa which he wore on his neck and prayed for help, for a miracle, for only a miracle could save him.

According to the folk tradition, Mary heard the supplications of this poor soldier and came to his rescue. In the fading rays of a bloodshot sunset wrapped in autumn mists, he is said to have seen Our Lady crossing the field of battle in a dark red gown and a golden cloak on which there were the emblems of the Holy Passion, and with a royal crown on Her head. The Virgin's ecstatically beautiful face was inexpressibly sorrowful. Her sad eyes looked down from under half-closed eye-lids onto a White Eagle which the Mother of God clasped to Her bosom.

Bending over the wounded man, Mary promised him his health and that he would return to his native land. She also told him to have an image of Her made.

"Take a good look at Me," She is said to have told him, "so that in that image I may appear just as I look now. You will set that image up in a public place in your home parts. My people will pray before that image and shall draw many graces at My hands in the hardest times of trial."

After that vision night fell, and some people found the wounded Tomasz in the bushes. Pitying him, they took him back to their house, called a doctor and patiently attended to him. Thanks to this he recuperated his strength and returned to health. In the spring of 1814 Tomasz Kłossowski returned home and settled at Izabelin, 7 kilometres from Licheń. He set up his blacksmith's shop again to earn his living by the sweat of his brow. He lived frugally and saved what money he could, which he would put aside for a pilgrimage on foot once a year for a whole month to a holy place. He remembered about Our Lady's instructions.

In gratitude for the saving of his life, the devout blacksmith searched and searched for the right picture for many years, but in vain. He went to many famous places of pilgrimage, renowned monasteries and churches; he saw a great many images of the Holy Virgin, but he never came across the beautiful, sorrowing face he had seen, which had become impressed on his mind's eye.

In 1836 Tomasz went on a walking pilgrimage to Częstochowa, for the Feast of the Nativity of the Blessed Virgin Mary, 8th September. He went to confession and received Holy Communion. He prayed and complained to Our Lady that he could not fulfil Her wish, as he had spent so many years searching for the right image in vain.

On his return journey on 9th September, when he had covered just 9 kilometres, at the village of Ligota he noticed that a group of pilgrims who were also returning from the celebrations had stopped for prayers before a wayside chapel put up on a tree in a field, just off the road. He joined them, and when they had finished and left he approached the shrine to find that picture in it was the one he had been looking for such a long time.

It had an image of the Virgin painted in oils on a larchen board. Her face was beautiful but also full of a sorrowing reflection. From under half-closed eye-lids Her sad eyes looked down onto a White Eagle with its wings spread out on Her bosom. Her sad look penetrated deep into Tomasz's heart.

Her countenance was full of serenity, majesty, and contemplation; it had grief in it but at the same time was full of goodness and a trusting hope. Her golden cloak carried the emblems of the Passion: the crown of thorns; the whips, the nails, and the spear. On her head there was a royal crown. At the Eagle's feet there was an inscription: "Queen of Poland, grant peace to our days."

The condition the painting was in showed that it was not new; it had been made decades before, perhaps even during the Confederation of Bar against the Russian invaders in 1772, when holy pictures would be painted in this manner.

Our Lady appears to Tomasz Kłossowski on the battlefield at Leipzig, 1813

←

Who had painted it? Who had hung it up on this tree? He did not know. But happy and deeply moved, Tomasz dropped down on his knees and, trembling with emotion, he stayed there with his eyes glued to the sacred countenance. A wave of memories now flooded his heart and it seemed to him that he was once more on the battlefield, exhausted, alone, and awaiting death, and that the Virgin was bending down over him, stretching out Her maternal arms to him. But why was She so anguished? Maybe because She was looking at the terrible instruments of torture which had rent Her beloved Son's body.

At that moment another idea flashed through his head. Mary was looking deep into his heart and soul, and She could see his sins and his weakness! That was what was causing Her such unspeakable pain! The pain and tears a Mother weeps over a bad child! Finally he felt that the spears piercing the heart of the Blessed Virgin, Queen of Poland, were the sins and unfaithfulness of the entire Polish nation.

The devout blacksmith watched, prayed, and whispered: "O, Blessed Virgin, I shall not leave this place without You; I must take You with me to my home parts."

Some people who were digging potatoes on the neighbouring patch told Tomasz that the field, tree, and painting were owned by a German colonist who had purchased the land some years earlier and settled there.

This German was a Protestant and he readily gave the picture to Tomasz. He told him that the picture had come to be hung on the tree one night, and that ever since then his field was being trampled by all the people on their way to or from Częstochowa and stopping before the picture, kneeling down, praying, and creeping around it on their knees. Nothing would grow on the field. So he was pleased to give the picture to Tomasz, asking for no money in return. Overjoyed, Tomasz took the painting down from the poplar-tree, bought a piece of linen cloth from a farmer's wife, wrapped the picture in it, pressed it to his bosom, and took it home to Izabelin.

For eight years the painting hung in Kłossowski's house, and was accorded reverence and veneration. Legend says that during this time the Madonna's face was occasionally bathed in sweat. People said that this was a sign, but the blacksmith had no intention of parting with the likeness of the Madonna, which he had come to love so much. People gossiped that the blacksmith must have had some secret sins on his conscience, since even the image of Our Lady felt ill at ease in his house. No wonder, they said, he had been a soldier and wandered far and wide, and of course everyone knew that soldiers were no saints.

Tomasz knew exactly what Our Lady wanted. He would delicately wipe away the drops of perspiration from her face with a towel, but he kept his secret from people and had no intention whatsoever of moving the picture out of his house, not even into a church.

In 1844 the blacksmith fell seriously ill. Neither the physician from Konin nor any sort of medicine helped. It seemed his death was near. The priest was called, and his neighbours came. Father Florian Kosiński, the parish priest, heard the sick man's confession and administered the holy oils. Tomasz was so weakened by his illness that he did not have the strength even to make the sign of the cross. When the priest and his neighbours had left, and Tomasz's wife was in the yard tending to her duties, Tomasz was left alone in the room.

Suddenly he heard a strange voice from the picture, "Tomasz, take Me out of this house into the forest."

In terror, Tomasz replied, "Blessed Virgin, how can I take You out of this house when I am so ill and weak I cannot stand up on my feet. Forgive me, Holy Mother Mary, but I cannot take you out of here."

"You will recover your health," he heard the mysterious voice say.

And at that instant a strange current ran through his entire body and he felt much better. He jumped out of bed, dressed, and ran out into the yard. Seeing this his wife shrieked, and people came rushing in, astonished to see that Tomasz, who had been almost dying an hour before, was now so cheerful and in perfect health. They asked what had happened. He told them that the Blessed Virgin restored his health but that he had to take Her image out into the forest.

On the next day the blacksmith went to a carpenter in Konin and ordered a small chapel for the painting. In a few days it was ready. It was brought to Izabelin by a certain Mertowski, Kłossowski's neighbour. Tomasz was sad to carry out the likeness of the Holy Virgin into the Forest of Grąblin. He borrowed a ladder from Farmer Machowczyk of Grąblin, he found a mighty pine hundreds of years old by a footpath, and on it, high above the road, he put up the shrine. Every Sunday, as he went to church and then on his way home, he would turn into the thicket to warm his heart and eyes with the sight of the Blessed Virgin. The old soldier would spend a long time there talking to the Holy Mother.

Tomasz died on 7th August 1848. He is still remembered as a great patriot and a good man, with a devotion to the Blessed Virgin. In 1967 the people of Izabelin put up a new tomb for him near the church on the slope of Licheń Hill, on the site of the tomb which had been devastated by the Nazis during the War.

THE PLACE WHERE POLAND BEGAN

Greater Poland and Cuiavia, and the towns of Kruszwica, Mogilno, Gniezno, Poznań, Konin lie on great plains, amid fertile and sandy fields, post-glacial lakes, broad meadows and deep forests. It was here that centuries ago the Polish State started. It was here that over a thousand years ago the light of the Gospel came to the country, and the Saviour's Cross was erected on Polish soil. Here the forefathers of Poland first heard the sweet name of Mary, Mother of God, and came to love Her with their warm, Slavonic hearts.

This is where what the people of Poland are today started. Here the loving eyes of the Queen of Heaven and of Poland first looked upon those generations enthralled in the slavery perpetrated by their neighbours and by their own sins. Mary decided to descend from heaven and come to the aid this land and its oppressed inhabitants, Her children.

And that is what happened.

***

Mikołaj Sikatka, born in Grąblin in 1787, used to graze cattle in the Grąblin Forest. He had spent his entire life in his home village, working on the estate owned by Count Kwielecki first as a stable-boy, then as a steward, and in his old age as a cowherd tending the cattle of both squire and peasants. He was married and had two sons.

There was nothing special about him either in his private life or at work. But with decent people he enjoyed a reputation as an honest, pious, prudent, and truthful man. He was said to be deeply religious and virtuous. Julian Wieniawski, a writer who knew him personally, described Mikołaj in his memoirs for 1852:

"He was a man of great honesty and a sweetness which is rare among peasants. This grey-haired old man's memories went back into the pre-revolutionary times; he could remember several generations of squires and the family trees of almost all of the peasant families in the village. He lived a pious and exemplary life, he kept away from taverns and tales; on the contrary, he would spread concord, peace, and charity."

Mikołaj tended cattle not only for the local landlord, but also of the peasants. In return the farmer's wives would offer him food, breakfast and supper in their houses, and they would send out a midday meal to him in the forest. While he grazed the cattle Mikołaj would say the rosary or tell his beads. From time to time he would come to the thicket where the image of the Virgin hung and there he would pray. He would wipe cobwebs away from the picture, he would deck it out with flowers, he would look after the place. After the death of Kłossowski the blacksmith he was probably the only person who knew of the woodland shrine and paid his respects there. And he was the one Our Lady chose for her messenger. He was the one to be entrusted with Her message from Heaven.

In August 1850 the excited cowherd started telling people that a most extraordinary woman had appeared to him on several occasions in the forest near the picture on the pine-tree. People were astonished to hear this story, they conjectured that the woman was the Blessed Virgin Mary Herself. The cowherd testified to these apparitions under oath before Father Kosiński, the parish priest, who was an honest and prudent clergyman, not given to exaltation, and hence his statements, views and opinions are absolutely trustworthy.

In an official letter dated 5th September 1852, to the General Consistory at Kalisz, Father Kosinski described the apparitions to Mikołaj the cowherd in the following way:

"For a few years in the Parish of Licheń there has been a picture of Our Lady in a wood near the village of Grąblin. It was affixed to a pine-tree by one of the parishioners, now deceased. For two years now, in that wood near the picture a cowherd from the said village has been seeing an unknown person who seems to be from another world and who has been endeavouring through the mediation of that cowherd to encourage the local people sincerely to do penance and to change their lives, which hitherto have been blameworthy in many respects, and who has told him to collect an offering for three Masses from this parish, to beg God to turn away the imminent threat of punishment and disease hanging over the wicked. This stranger has also been admonishing him that the picture should be removed from that place in the wilds over a footpath to another, safer spot, where it would be protected against the insults of the impious which might occur in the forest away from the eyes of witnesses and with impunity. She is said to

Our Lady appears to Mikołaj Sikatka the cowherd, 1850

have repeated this instruction and exhortation several times. The said cowherd, when questioned before the bailiff of the local authority at Gosławice gave the same testimony, which was taken down in a report. Subsequently, when he was sent to appear before the captain of Konin, again he produced the same evidence."

This is all that Father Kosiński's official document says of the momentous events that took place in the years 1850-1852 in the Parish of Licheń. The letter is brief, but it contains all the salient aspects of the apparitions, what happened to the cowherd, and to the picture of the Blessed Virgin.

The letter was written at a time when there was already a conflict between Mikołaj Sikatka and the parish priest over the erection of a chapel on the site of the apparitions, work on which had already started. That is why it is so laconic and does not even mention the cowherd's name. The letter deliberately made no mention of all the patriotic aspects and prophecies concerning the future of Poland. Father Kosiński neither had the right nor the wish to conduct an interrogation of this visionary without the consent of his spiritual authority. He left the entire matter, which was rather embarrassing and dangerous with respect to the Partitioners' civil authorities, to the decision of his superiors.

But it is thanks to this letter, and also to the diverse publications which came out in the Austrian and Prussian partitional zones on the matter immediately after the events and later, as well as to the still living local tradition that we are able to reproduce well-nigh the full details of the story of Our Lady's apparitions and of the origins of the cult of the Miraculous Picture of Our Lady of Licheń.

THE BEGINNING OF THE APPARITIONS

The cowherd Mikołaj saw Our Lady for the first time in early May, 1850, and this is how it all began:

It was nearly midday. The cattle had had its fill of the rich spring grass and was now resting in the meadow, while the cowherd, as was his custom, was kneeling on a dry tuft of grass and saying the rosary. It was a warm and sunny day, full of the scent of spring flowers. The birds in the trees, which had been chirping away merrily since morning, now hushed. While he was praying, Mikołaj noticed that a woman dressed in the ordinary way like all the other women of the village was approaching him. She had a long, pale gown, a and a white scarf on her head. As she approached him, she greeted him with the following words:

"Praised be Jesus Christ."

"Amen," said the cowherd, convinced it was one of the farmer's wives bringing his midday meal. But when he took a closer look at Her, he saw that She was not one of the Grąblin women that he knew. Her face had an extraordinary beauty about it. Confused by this unexpected encounter, the cowherd stood in silence.

Then the stranger said to him, "Mikołaj, tell people that God's retribution for their sins is at hand. An infectious disease will trouble the entire population of the locality. Thousands of people will die suddenly in the fields and in their houses. Encourage them to do penance and to pray; if they repent, the punishment will be averted. Let them pray especially by saying the rosary and contemplating the life and Passion of Jesus."

Saying these words the Lady showed Mikołaj a long rosary of fifteen mysteries.

"People have been depraved. If they do not repent, soon there will come a terrible war, and many will suffer. There will come a contagious disease, and many will suffer and die of it. Mikołaj, I ask you to attend to the holy picture on the pine, for all the people will come here and draw a stream of graces through it."

After these words the strange Lady was silent. For some time She stood there very sad and full of suffering, almost weeping. She took another sorrowful glance at the cowherd and started to move away. Mikołaj noticed that as She moved her feet did not

The hill in Grąblin Forest where Our Lady appeared

touch the soft meadow, but glided over the grass on a shiny golden cloud. His heart trembled as he suddenly realised that the person he had before his eyes was not of this world. He fell to his knees and stretched out his arms. He wanted to shout but could not. The beautiful Lady stopped just for a moment, and then it was all gone in the bright rays of the midday sunlight.

When the cowherd had recovered his composure, there was not a soul in sight over the entire meadows. The herd was chewing over its fodder, and there was calmness and tranquillity in the warm air. The Angelus bell was being rung from Licheń Church.

As he knelt, said his prayers and recited the rosary in his mind's eye he could still see the Lady and hear her sad voice. Then he made his way to the pine-tree in the wood and meticulously tidied up the entire surroundings of the tree, picking up all the branches, twigs, and dead leaves that had fallen there, sprinkled fresh sand, and enclosed it in a ring of stones. He decked the shrine with the image of Our Lady with fresh flowers and green branches. He said a prayer and returned to the cattle. In the evening he drove the herd back to the village, excited by what he had seen and heard at noon. But he was afraid of malicious folk and their mocking tongues, so he told no-one about the apparition, nor did he encourage anyone to do penance. He devoted a great deal of his time himself to prayer, both during the day and at night. He fasted, did penance, and would go to the shrine in the forest more and more often, spending a good deal of time there on fervent prayer. He never parted with his rosary even for a moment. His fingers told the beads, and his lips mouthed the Paters and Aves, his heart sank into the unfathomed mysteries of the Incarnation, the Redemption, and the Glory of the Son of God and His Immaculate Mother.

One of the apparitions took place while Mikołaj was kneeling before the woodland shrine, saying the rosary. He was gazing into

*T*omb of the visionary Mikołaj Sikatka

the Virgin's beautiful face, when suddenly he heard the footsteps of someone coming up to him. He turned around and saw a Lady approaching him along the woodland path from Grąblin. She was dressed in white robes and in Her hand carried a basket into which She put the sylvan flowers She was picking. Her extraordinary beauty and the bright rays which enveloped Her showed that She came from another world. When he saw Her he fell to his knees. The Blessed Virgin stopped in front of him and rebuked him for not having called people to penance and prayer. Then She again spoke of the impending wrath of God:

"People have become bad; they are offending God with grave sins. My Son is very angry; He will punish the guilty very severely. I am begging My Son to refrain for a while still and have mercy, but I can no longer hold off His just retribution. Unless the people repent and do penance, there will come a heavy scourge of punishment on them; they will die of a plague. Soon a terrible, long war will ravage the whole of Europe. The sea will be red with blood. Very many people will perish. The desperate weeping of the widows and orphans will be heard."

Our Lady was foretelling the Crimean War, which was about to break out and which shook the mighty Russian Empire, bringing hope to the men and women of Poland of liberty from their partitioners' yoke. But the nation did not take full advantage of this opportunity. The January Uprising, which came later, in 1863, when Russia had already recovered after her losses and her defeat at the hands of Turkey, no longer had the same chance of success.

"Let the people recite the rosary and beg God for mercy," said Mary. "You shall go round the neighbourhood and collect offerings for Masses of expiation. Let everyone, including the poorest, make an offering for alms. Let the priests say Masses begging God to avert the imminent retribution on the wicked for their evil ways. Whenever priests and congregations come before God with the Most Holy Body and Blood of Christ in their hands they will always succeed in obtaining mercy, forgiveness of sins, and the grace of blessing. Masses are what saves sinners. So let the people listen to their priests and suffer not to be parted from them, for then it will be lost and perish."

"O, my priests, pray and bless the people, always bless the people. Do not complain at them, do not become discouraged, bless them always. I am the most loving and caring of mothers for every priest. If he prays and does penance I shall lift him up and cleanse him; I shall strengthen and protect him; I shall fill his heart with joy. Multitudes of priests will come to this place; here I shall endow them with special graces; here they will recover their constancy of spirit and their pristine zeal. My sons, here I shall always await you; here I shall look out for you."

After these words for a while Mary gazed at the picture in the shrine, and then She said:

"Mikołaj, make efforts to have this image accorded reverence and protection against the insults of those whose faith is poor. Let all the people do penance, and God Himself will lead them along the way of the cross and glory. If there is no general improvement in their lives, repentance for sins, unity amongst brethren; if the people are not converted to God again, then new terrible suffering and oppression will fall on this miserable land. Its best sons will die in battle, betrayed and forsaken by false allies. Some will never again see the light of day in dungeons; the bones of others will languish in exile. Mothers and wives will wear lifelong widow's weeds. A time of great trial will come for the Church's faithfulness. The walls of churches will be spattered with the blood of their defenders. Children will be tortured for their mother tongue. The fold will be pulled apart and scattered, and its shepherds put in chains. They will be the first to undergo vicious suffering, but I shall always afford them perseverance; they shall never be traitors of the faith, the Church, or of the people. The priests who are to emerge from this people shall accomplish great signs and works; they shall be admired by the whole world."

Having said these words, the Blessed Virgin cast Her profoundly sad gaze upon the cowherd, and then She was enveloped in a brilliant light in which She vanished.

Our Lady's message of sorrow lay like a huge weight on the meek and modest cowherd's heart. He knew that he had to divulge all of these things that he had seen and heard; but he also knew he would be running the risk of people's ridicule, hardship and persecution. Who would believe him that he had seen the Virgin Mary? Who would take Her summons to penance to heart and transform his sinful life? How was he to prove the truthfulness of his words? It was beyond his powers. He redoubled his own prayers and penitential practices. He received the sacraments; and he looked after the holy picture on the pine-tree; and so the weeks passed but he never divulged his secret to anyone.

August 15th of that year was an exceptionally fine day. The soil, which had been parched by a hot summer, at last received the rain it so needed, which came in a heavy downpour lasting the whole of the vigil of the Feast of the Assumption. After midnight the rain stopped, and a light breeze dispersed the remnants of the clouds. A bright refreshing morning rose, full of the fragrance of the flowers and herbs people were bringing into church for the traditional blessing of the flowers. The old cowherd enviously watched his neighbours in their Sunday best on their way to Licheń Church for High Mass. That day it was his turn of duty minding the cattle; he could not leave the herd and, like the others, attend the special service in honour of the Assumption of Our Lady. It was nearly noon, and the well-grazed animals were lying on the grass in the shadow of the trees, while Mikołaj made his way to the pine-tree as he usually did and there sang the praises of Mary with hymns and the recitation of the rosary. He gazed for a long time at the sweet face of the Virgin in the image on the pine-tree, and it seemed to him that he was to blame for that agony in it. He was to blame, for he was silent, he was afraid, he cared more about what people would think and say than about the works of God.

"Dear Mother of God, do not be angry with me," the old man whispered, "but You can see for Yourself how little people pay attention to me. Who will believe me, who will listen to a village

Chapel marking the place of Our Lady's last apparition, Grąblin

cowherd? My efforts will be in vain; I won't convert anybody; they'll only call me a madman and I'll have a hard time."

So he prayed and wept, he wiped away the tears and whispered his prayers, and then he climbed up the nearby hill to see if the herd had not scattered over the wood. The animals were resting in their old place. Slowly the old man climbed down from the hill and stood on the side of the road to Grąblin and Licheń. At this time of day it was empty. The people were not yet on their way back from church. And suddenly it was as if a new sun had been set ablaze above the entire forest. The cowherd turned and saw what seemed to be a sphere flashing with rays of light streaming down from the blue sky over the wood and suddenly stopping over the trees on the hill. The brightness started moving towards him and stopped just above the road. The astonished Mikołaj covered his half-blinded eyes with his arms, and when after a while he removed them from his face and looked out, his knees bent under him. He saw the exquisitely beautiful figure of the Blessed Mother of God. She was dressed in a dark red gown with a white waist-band, and a white and gold cloak flowing down in folds from Her head, over Her shoulders and down to Her feet. On the edges of Her cloak were the emblems of the Holy Passion. On Her head there was a costly crown; Her delicate hand held a White Eagle to Her bosom. In Her other hand there was a long rosary. Her youthful face was full of a sorrowful contemplation.

"The Sorrowful Queen of Poland," the idea flashed through Mikołaj's mind, "the same one as in the holy picture on the pine-tree." As he knelt gazing up, trembling out of happiness and excitement, Mary began Her prophecies:

"People are committing sins, they have no thought of repentance and changing their lives. Not much time will pass and God will punish them severely. A terrible plague will visit the country, and many will die of it. They will perish suddenly; there will be no-one to bury their bodies. Old people and infants at their mothers' breasts will die. Young men and maidens will be punish-

*W*oodland shrine of Our Lady in the Grąblin Forest

ed; little orphans will mourn their parents. Then there will come a long and cruel war. Millions will die."

After this terrible prophecy the Blessed Virgin was silent. Her face was clouded by an inexpressible sorrow and pain; tears stood in Her eyes. Seeing those days full of grief and horror in Her mind's eye, She was anguished for Her people. Her maternal heart was pierced by a sharp sword. After a while, as if wishing to leave a ray of hope for a rescue for Her people, She continued:

"The Heavenly Father's Mercy is inexhaustible. Everything can still be averted. If the people have saints, all may yet be saved. The people need holy mothers... I love your good mothers. I shall always come to their help in all adversities. I understand them: I was a deeply sorrowing mother... Your persecutors' most perfidious intents will be frustrated by your mothers. They will give the nation many heroic children, who in a time of worldwide conflagration will win freedom for their country..."

"Satan will sow the seeds of discord among brethren. Your wounds will not yet have healed, a generation will not have passed when the earth, sky and sea again will flow with blood so profusely as never before. This land will be soaked with tears, ashes, and the blood of martyrs for a sacred cause. Throughout the country young people will sacrifice their lives for it. Innocent children will be slain by the sword. These new, innumerable martyrs will intercede at God's mercy-throne on your behalf when the ultimate battle comes for the Nation's soul, when judgement will be passed on you. In the crucible of long-lasting tribulation your faith will purified; your hope shall not be extinguished; your love shall not fail you. I shall walk among you; I shall protect you; I shall help you, and through you the world. To the amazement of all the nations of the world, the hope of all the oppressed peoples shall arise from Poland."

"Then all hearts shall be moved by a joy the like of which there has not been for a thousand years. That will be the greatest sign given to the Nation for its conversion and its confirmation. That sign will unite you. Then exceptional graces, the like of which there has not been for a thousand years, shall stream down on this troubled and humiliated land."

"Young hearts will be moved. The seminaries and the convents will be full to the brim. Polish hearts will carry the faith east and west, north and south. The peace of God will ensue."

"Mikołaj, tell people of this; rebuke and console them. Do penance and be vigilant. When those hard days for the people come, when sorrow fills your hearts, those who come to this picture to pray and do penance shall not perish; they shall be comforted and saved. They shall have their sick bodies and souls healed. I shall build a deep well; they will drink of its refreshing water, and their hearts shall be filled with joy. If the Polish Nation improves, it shall be comforted, saved, and lifted up, an example to other nations. Satan will fight against it in all manner whatsoever, so as to prevent its revival, but the final victory shall be with Me. Here, where the light of the faith in salvation was first brought, My light for revival and raising up from sin shall be set up. Do not let the dragon of hell deceive you; keep faith with God. I shall cover you with My mantle and protect you from mortal danger."

"I shall never fail this Nation whenever it turns to Me for assistance; I shall defend it and press it to My heart as I now do with the White Eagle."

"Let this image, which now hangs on a pine-tree in a woodland thicket, be transferred to a fitting place and honoured publicly, so that it be safe against insult from irreverent people. People from all over Poland will come here to My image, and here they will be comforted in their severe tribulations. I shall reign over my people throughout the ages. Sooner or later a magnificent church will be built in this place in My honour."

"If it is not built by people, I shall send angels to set it up. Here on this spot there will be a monastery built, and My sons will serve Me in it. There will be a straight road between this place and Baniszewo."

Main altar in the Ostra Brama Chapel, with the Image of Our Lady of Ostra Brama

"Mikołaj, you will suffer much, but do not be put off, spread abroad what you have seen and heard. To make people believe you, I shall make you young."

Upon these words Mikołaj's milk-white hair and beard turned black, and his old withered face was suddenly a young man's fresh and healthy face. The cowherd knelt dumbfounded, observing all these celestial wonders. His heart beat fast, and a strange power and steadfast courage entered his soul. He was now full of zeal to go out into the land telling people to reform their lives, to stop sinning and incurring God's anger, otherwise God's patience would come to an end and He would punish His obstinate children. He was now ready to get up and go into his village telling the people to improve and to stop sinning. Had their country not been sundered enough by the Partitioners, he would ask them, did they not have enough with the **chains of slavery** and humiliation? Could they not understand? Why were they making their Heavenly Mother weep?

"O, Sorrowful Queen of Poland, be comforted and do not weep any longer; I shall not hold back any longer, I shall go forth and carry out Your command; You shall be honoured in this impoverished locality of Licheń," the lips and heart of this god-fearing cowherd whispered, while the Blessed Virgin looked down on him with grace and affection.

And suddenly the Virgin Most Pure was enveloped in a golden light. Heaven seemed to open before the cowherd's eyes. He saw Mary in a human majesty of glory. She shone in might and glory as the Queen of Heaven, Queen of the World, and Queen of Poland. Then a new wave of golden light enclosed the figure of the Blessed Virgin. She was covered with the glistening of

M ain altar in the Church of Our Lady of Częstochowa, Licheń, with the Image of the Black Madonna

a thousand hues in the still air, and then She rose up high above the forest into the bright azure of the sky.

The heavenly apparition had long since disappeared, but Mikołaj was still kneeling with his arms outstretched, as if he wanted to make this beautiful vision stay longer. He was praying and pledging his fidelity to Mary.

It was in this posture that the people returning from High Mass in Licheń Church found him. Amazed, they crowded round the old man who had suddenly regained his youth and started asking what he had seen.

Then he told them that for several months already he had been seeing a strange, brightly clad person in the woods, and that She had been there again that day, that Her footsteps could still be made out in the sand... He told them how the Lady had prophesied the approaching divine retribution, and that She called them to prayer and penance, and honour for Her holy image on the pine-tree.

Word went round the village and its environs fast that the Virgin Mary had appeared to Mikołaj the cowherd. But in vain did he exhort the people to penance and prayer; in vain he told them what he had seen and heard. His words were not believed. Just like today, people then were not eager to do penance, so they preferred to treat Mikołaj's relation with incredulity rather than be converted and abandon their sinful ways.

They were insulting God by their drinking and unchaste lives, their swearing and quarrelling, their marital infidelities and infringements of holy days. Few people prayed, but instead gossip, calumny and discord were the order of the day. Churches were half-empty during services, and there would be no-one to carry the holy picture during processions, but instead in every village the taverns were packed full and bursting at the seams with revelry. The affluent nobility and gentry had become inordinately bold and arrogant, and were mercilessly oppressing their peasants. Sometimes they would pay their labourers for the hard work on their estates in alcohol, not in money or crops. Godless women would distil moonshine in their houses, and then sell it cheaply not only to adults, but to adolescents as well.

There were no schools, no books, there was no education... Obscurity reigned in worldly affairs and in religion... The afflicted people led miserable lives and sought relief in alcohol and sins of the flesh. There was no respect for older people. Sons would raise their arms against their fathers. Mothers would weep because of their unchaste daughters, who would drown their illegitimate offspring in the village pond before dressing in a white gown and veil, as if in mockery, to be married in church. Instead of believing in God, they would put their faith in superstition, magic, and witches.

This was happening in the towns, villages, and in the lords' estates. It was happening in the Parish of Licheń, too, perhaps it was worse there than elsewhere. It seemed that the devil himself, who had once in pagan times been worshipped on Licheń Hill but had been cast out by the Cross, had returned and was again instituting his rule. There was no concern for the House of God; priests were denigrated and treated with disrespect. People did not pray much, and did not attend religious services very often, even though they lived a stone's throw away from the church.

It got so bad that robberies and satanic sacrileges would be committed in this poor church. The Blessed Sacrament was scattered all over the church. Even the saintly parish priest, Father Florian Kosiński, could not move the hardened hearts of the inhabitants of Licheń, and persuade them to change their evil ways.

In 1845 the old wooden church reached such a state of dilapidation that it collapsed. Father Kosiński collected what could still be of service out of the rotting timber and put up a small chapel in the graveyard to say Mass in it. The following year he set about the construction of a new brick-built church. There was a ceremony for the blessing of its foundation stone, and that marked the end of the building scheme. Neither entreaties nor threats, nor even ardent prayer helped. People's hearts were like cold stones. They did not

*E*ntry of Our Lady of Licheń, the Sorrowful Queen, 1852

want to contribute any money for the church fund, or help in the work on the building site. No progress could be made.

Seeing that the parishioners were not keen to have a new church built, the parish's patroness, Countess Izabela Kwilecka, made no special efforts to proceed with the project without the people's assistance and concern. There was money for food and drink, for amusements and fancy clothes, but not a penny for the church. There was time for everything, but not for work on the building of the church. This was happening in Licheń, but also throughout the whole land. The partitioning powers deliberately kept the Poles in ignorance; they were pleased to observe a decline in their spiritual acumen, wholesome morality, national culture and ambitions of regaining independence. The best people in Poland had either perished in the numerous wars and uprisings, or were languishing in the prisons. Thousands of patriotic individuals were exiles and were wandering through foreign lands, in vain seeking assistance from their kings and princes for their hapless country. The hardest blows had fallen on its spiritual leaders, the bishops, priests, monks, and on the entire Catholic Church. The Primate and many of the bishops and priests were in prison. The activities of others were hampered. Monasteries and seminaries were being closed down. In the Germanised schools of the Prussian Partition children were punished very severely for speaking their native language; some were even beaten for this. In this situation some people were beginning to accept such a fate and to collaborate with the partitioning powers. In a word things were bad in the wretched country and in the poor, purblind hearts of its people. The wrath of God might easily have been expected, but people did not give this any thought.

The cowherd was ridiculed, along with his Virgin Mary who walked about in the woods and meadows calling people to penance. When Mikołaj would not stop calling people to reform their lives, he was accused before the Russian police of spreading unrest among the people and telling them unheard of things about a Virgin Mary with a White Eagle on Her bosom. Soon policemen came to Grąblin, arrested the cowherd, and took him off for an interrogation to the local bailiff at Gosławice. The bailiff, Marcin Sucharski, gave Mikołaj an official hearing, wrote a report, and issued an order for Mikołaj to be sent to the local *Powiat* authorities in Konin. The captain of the military authority in the *Powiat* of Konin was a Zabłocki, a severe man, the terror of the neighbourhood. Interrogations before him lasted a long time. When, in spite of threats, Mikołaj persisted in claiming that he had seen the Virgin Mary, Captain Zabłocki had the visionary cast into prison and tortured. In prison Mikołaj's black tresses and beard — a tangible sign that something had happened to him which could not be explained by a natural cause, something which made him look young despite his 65 years of age — were shaved off.

When the elaborate tortures did not break his spirit, the prison doctor was summoned to Mikołaj. The doctor, who was in police pay, cut Mikołaj's veins on his temples and both of his wrists. The very weak and half-dying cowherd was then kept in a dungeon, while the doctor issued a diagnosis which said that Mikołaj was suffering from a psychiatric disorder.

The police published a statement on the grounds of the doctors' report that there had been no apparitions of the Virgin Mary in Grąblin Wood, and that the old cowherd was a liar, charlatan, and mentally ill. People in the entire *Gubernya* of Kalisz read these public announcements. Priests did not mention the matter at all. Many first learned of Grąblin and the apparitions to a cowherd only now.

What the partitional authorities were most afraid of was the fact that the image of the Virgin Mary both in the woodland shrine and in the apparitions carried a White Eagle — the revered emblem of the Poles. They thought there were political motives, some sort of incitement to an uprising against the Muscovite oppressors, hidden behind the whole affair.

One more misfortune was to visit the cowherd. During his imprisonment his wife went out into the woods with a bundle of twigs and branches on her back; she had a heart attack, fell on the footpath and died. Irreverent people took this as an opportune sign, they said it was the punishment of God on liars and charlatans. Nobody had ever heard of the Virgin Mary appearing to a mean cowherd. It was quite different with devout nuns or innocent children, but not to a married man with children.

GOD'S PUNISHMENT COMES

In August 1852 a terrible epidemic of cholera, which Mary had foretold, broke out in Poland and all over Europe. The disease decimated the old, young people, and children. It struck suddenly, with a strong head-ache, distressing vomiting, and dysentery. Patients thought their internal organs were on fire, and they were so thirsty that they would crawl to the nearest well, puddle, or ditch, drank the water there, went blue in the face and died in terrible pain. Whole families perished, large settlements turned into ghost-towns.

God's patience had been exhausted. He sent punishment on the sinners. Absolutely powerless and terrified people fled to the woods, marshes, and other inaccessible places. There was no-one to bury the dead. Stray dogs, wild cats and birds devoured human corpses and spread the contagion even more.

At Licheń the parish priest ordered a deep ditch dug in the corner of the graveyard and prepared a supply of quicklime. Every day a couple of men went round the villages with a cart, and would drag the bodies of the dead into the cart with iron hooks and bring them to the graveyard. Here the corpses were thrown into the ditch, strewn with quicklime, and covered with earth. The dead would not be dressed for burial, as it was feared the healthy could be infected in this way. Houses in which no inhabitants were left would have their doors barred with planks nailed to them, and a cross would be painted on them with whitewash to show that the plague had visited the place.

In that time of catastrophe, panic and helplessness people started to return to God, begging Him for deliverance. They flocked to church for the Sacrament of Penance and Holy Communion; they vowed to change their lives and had masses said for themselves. No-one could be certain that he and his family would live to see the next day. Seeing what was happening, the authorities freed Mikołaj from prison. People started believing that he had been telling the truth. Only then did they remember that Our Lady had told them the image in the forest would be the last hope of those suffering punishment, the afflicted and the dying.

The place where the Blessed Virgin had stood during Her last apparition was separated off by a small fence. People would show each other Her alleged footprints in the middle of the patch. Next to this enclosure two farmers from the village of Trzyboki, Szymon Łebkowski and Józef Pękasiewicz, set about building a brick chapel at their own expense. The place was called Dąbrówka. When the chapel was ready, they decided to put the image of the Madonna that hung on the pine inside the new building.

On 23rd August 1852 they transferred the picture without informing the parish priest of the matter. From that day onwards crowds of pilgrims not only from the neighbourhood, but also from the whole country and even from abroad started flocking to the image in the chapel. Day and night people kept vigil there in prayer and supplication. Miracles started to happen. Seriously ill people would suddenly be cured here. The people acknowle''red the miraculous power of this image of the Blessed Virgin. ﹍y finally believed that the cowherd Mikołaj had indeed had true visions.

The sick would be brought here; mothers would bring their dying children; infected people crept to the holy picture. People confessed their sins, beat their breast, and vowed to be better, they would stretch out their arms and call out desperately, "Mother of God, save us! O, Sorrowful Queen of Poland, comfort us!" They would creep round the chapel on their knees; they would lie prostrate. Strange things that had never happened before now happened before the likeness of the Comfort of the Distressed. All the sick and those with fever had their health restored, and the dying their lives. Even those who were brought here on carts in their death-throes would be cured miraculously and would walk away and return to their homes happy.

News of all this spread like wildfire through the land. No wonder that day by day more and more people of all estates and different religions arrived from distant parts in Grąblin Wood at the place of the apparitions and miracle cures. Alongside Catholics, Protestants and Russian Orthodox Christians, and even Jews came to pray there. The terrible disease spared no-one, and a sick and suffering person is ready to try anything that can help. All of them without exception were miraculously assisted by Mary, the best of mothers.

Crucifix in the Holy Cross Chapel, which Bertha Bauer damaged by gunfire

THE BISHOP'S COMMISSION

Father Florian Kosiński, parish priest of Licheń, sent detailed reports relating all of these incidents to his ecclesiastic authorities at Kalisz. At the same time he asked for advice and a decision on how he was to behave in the situation. Bishop Walenty Mateusz Tomaszewski and his General Consistory sent a special commission to Licheń to examine the cowherd Mikołaj, the cured persons, and the picture itself. Under the chairmanship of Father Michał Odorowski, Dean of Sompolno, the Bishop's Commission arrived in Licheń on 5th September 1852. First the witnesses were heard in the parish presbytery at Licheń, then the Commission went to the forest to take a look for itself at what had been happening. The inspection irritated Dean Odorowski and the rest of the Commission. There was a huge crowd of worshippers around the little chapel with the Madonna's picture. People were kneeling or lying prostrate; they were praying and singing hymns; there was a mass of candles burning, and money being put into the collection-box near the shrine. Next to this piety the Commission also discovered a source of sin and corruption. Some depraved persons, Satan's servants, had set up barrels of alcohol next to the shrine, and were selling it to the pilgrims. They were encouraging people to buy their alcohol, which would protect them better against cholera than devout prayers before a little picture. People who had come from afar and were cold bought the alcohol and drank it, and then they would prostrate themselves in a state of stupor before the image of the Blessed Virgin Mary.

Through evil people Satan was pursuing his depraving business in the place where miracles had been wrought. He was contaminating the holy place with the sin of drunkenness.

Another matter that angered Father Kosiński and the Bishop's Commission was the fact that the people had started the erection of a large chapel in Grąblin Wood on their own. The foundations were ready, rocks and bricks were being transported now, mortar was being mixed, and a couple of bricklayers were building the walls. Pilgrims were depositing generous donations in the large padlocked collecting-box for the building fund for the chapel and a monastery for monks. The keys to this box were in the hands of lay people.

On Licheń Hill the foundation stone for the new parish church which had been consecrated seven years earlier had already been covered by moss, weeds and bracken, and neither the parishioners nor Countess Kwilecka had any intention of proceeding with the building scheme. Masses were said in the tiny graveyard chapel, which was cramped and uncomfortable. Father Kosiński had already lost hope of ever being able to continue the project. But here in the woods there was such enthusiasm and devotion to the cause of the chapel building project. If a monastery were to be founded here, it would mean the end of Licheń.

During the apparitions Our Lady had said that a magnificent church would be built here, in which Her image would be housed. The people wanted to carry out Mary's wish as quickly as possible. The Bishop's Commission could thus infer that Mikołaj the cowherd was furtively encouraging them. When Father Kosiński suggested the picture be moved into Licheń Church, the people were outraged. The inhabitants of Grąblin, Izabelin, and Anielewo, along with some of the pilgrims, said they would never permit the removal of the picture to Licheń and that they would erect a chapel in the forest. It seemed open warfare was about to break out over the picture of Our Lady which people held to be capable of working miracles. This was the background to the controversy between Father Kosiński and Mikołaj the cowherd.

Father Kosiński's will prevailed, and the Bishop summoned troops to keep the peace.

The picture was transferred to Licheń, as I am going to relate, while the cowherd was pushed into the background and the role he had played trivialised.

To this very day the foundations of the chapel the building of which was stopped by the Bishop stand amid the bracken in Grąblin Wood. Any who should dare disobey the Bishop's in-

W PRACY, CIERPIENIU
I ŚMIERCI ZOSTALIŚMY
WIERNI BOGU, KOŚCIOŁOWI
I OJCZYŹNIE

KAPLICĘ
MĘCZEŃNIKÓW I BOHATERÓW
POLSKIEGO NARODU
UROCZYŚCIE POŚWIĘCIŁ
KSIĄDZ KARDYNAŁ JÓZEF GLEMP
PRYMAS POLSKI
28 CZERWCA 1987 ROKU

SŁUGA BOŻY
KS. BP MICHAŁ KOZAL
MĘCZENNIK
UR. 25. 9. 1893 R.
PONIÓSŁ ŚMIERĆ MĘCZEŃSKĄ
DNIA 26. 1. 1943 R.
W OBOZIE KONCENTRACYJNYM
W DACHAU

BŁOGOSŁAWIONYM OGŁOSIŁ
NA PLACU DEFILAD W WARSZAWIE
PAPIEŻ POLAK
JAN PAWEŁ II
W CZASIE I KRAJOWEGO KONGRESU
EUCHARYSTYCZNEGO
DNIA 14 CZERWCA 1987 R.

National memorial wall, with monuments of Bishop Michał Kozal, who was killed in the Dachau concentration camp, and General Władysław Sikorski, wartime C-o-C of the Polish Forces

Memorial to Poles who died in the Katyn Massacre and elsewhere in the Soviet Union

junction were under the threat of ecclesiastic penalties and ana-themas.

People were so offended by the decision that the Bishop issued a pastoral letter to the congregations of his diocese explaining that it would be to the great glory of the Virgin Mary if Her image were venerated in a parish church. Priests reassured their parishioners, telling them that such a holy picture could not stay in the wild forest with no priests to look after it. It had to be moved from the forest to Licheń, and that was where a church should be built in honour of Our Lady.

After an inspection on the spot, the Dean sent a very detailed report to the Bishop, who gave an order for the image of the Blessed Virgin Mary which was generally considered to be charismatic and miraculous, to be transferred to the provisional parish church at Licheń, which was only 2 kilometres away from the site of the apparitions.

He also issued a dour letter to Countess Izabela Kwilecka, collatress of Licheń Church, warning her that unless she proceeded with the building of the church at Licheń immediately, he would bring a case against her before the authorities in Warsaw for serious negligence of duty.

THE ENTRY OF THE SORROWFUL QUEEN OF POLAND

On Sunday, 22nd September 1852 the Bishop of Kalisz and Cuiavia's letter was publicly read in all the churches of the diocese announcing the ceremonies for the transfer of the Miraculous Image of the Virgin Mary from Grąblin Wood to the temporary parish church at Licheń. After a long expostulation on the veneration of holy images in the Catholic Church, the Bishop wrote, "Whether or not this be to the liking of any person, the picture shall be transferred, as that is my will and command."

Sunday, 29th September 1852, the Feast of St. Michael the Archangel, was marked by a sign from heaven. From the early morning the day had been bright and sunny, calm without a cloud in the sky. Before 9 o'clock a strange, unearthly light appeared over the place where the apparitions had occurred. The phenomenon lasted for 2 hours. During the procession with the miraculous image golden flashes of lightning, but noiselessly, rent the sky from east to west. Very many priests, all the local *Powiat* authorities, and the supreme authorities of the *Gubernya* at Kalisz, including the Governor Prince Golitsyn, attended the translation ceremony. Numerous members of the gentry and aristocracy came to Licheń that day, along with about 80 thousand pilgrims. At 11 o'clock a procession set out from Licheń Church for the shrine in Grąblin Wood. There a service in honour of the Virgin Mary was celebrated and a sermon preached. Then Father Wałowski, parish priest of Mąkolno, removed the picture from the shrine and handed it over to two priests who carried it wrapped in a veil and under a canopy to Licheń. To prevent potential disorder and opposition from the inhabitants of Grąblin, on the Governor's order a police escort of 200 men surrounded the two priests who carried the holy picture. The procession was a magnificent, strange and somewhat symbolic sight. Our Lady the Sorrowful Queen of Poland was being carried to Her throne at Licheń, accompanied by a train which united Poles and Russians, Catholics alongside Orthodox Christians and Protestants and followers of Judaism. All those who were grateful for having been granted graces came. After 2 hours the procession reached Licheń Hill.

The picture was placed in the main altar of the wooden Church of Our Lady of Częstochowa. In the evening, after all the ceremonies had finished and the people had dispersed, it was removed to the presbytery for a commission to examine and draw up a report describing it.

The Governor and the Government Commission declared that this likeness of the Madonna could not be worshipped publicly because it carried overtly Polish national, patriotic attributes. This would have a bad effect on the attitudes of the Poles, who tended to be excessively patriotic and were continually stirring up rebellions against their Russian masters. It would be better if the picture were moved to Kalisz and deposited in the Governor's safe-keeping, or perhaps to Konin and kept by the military captain.

The Bishop's delegate and the Church Commission explained to Prince Golitsyn that the picture had no Polish patriotic attributes at all. The Madonna was holding the Holy Ghost in the form of a dove, not the crowned White Eagle of Poland. They seemed to be getting nowhere in trying to persuade the Russians, who continued to scrutinise the picture, when the door was flung open and four churchwardens came into the room carrying the heavy collection-box into which people had put donations for the building of the chapel. Father Kosiński asked the Commissions to open the box and count the money in it. There were copper, silver and gold coins in the box. After the money had been counted, the

Government Commission finally agreed to write in the official report that the Virgin in the painting carried a symbolic representation of the Holy Spirit in the form of a dove. The report never mentioned the donations collected in the box.

The image stayed in Licheń and could be placed in the main altar for public veneration, but below the picture of Our Lady of Częstochowa. The clock was striking midnight when the two commissions finished their work. The day in which a new holy place had been established on Polish territory was coming to an end.

The atmosphere of that day and its ceremonies had been so elevated that even now the local people talk about it describing the minutest details and adding fancy decorations. One of the things that are told is, for instance, that there was so much light coming from the picture that Father Wałowski was blinded by it and had to approach the shrine three times before he could remove the image. Another beautiful addition from local legend is that during the procession a dense shower of roses fell from the sky, giving the Blessed Virgin a lovely, thick carpet to move along.

On that memorable day the Holy Mother's wish was fulfilled. Her image was transferred to the beautiful hill at Licheń. She was exalted, and God had mercy on His penitent people and throughout the land the epidemic stopped. The Parish of Licheń, deeply moved by these events, immediately set about the building of a new brick church. Pilgrims contributed to the project, but most of the costs were covered by Countess Kwilecka and then, after her death, by her son Władysław Kwilecki, who completed the church and furnished it. On 18th October 1858 the Bishop of Kalisz, Bishop Marszewski, consecrated the new church at Licheń The celebrations lasted three days, during which the Bishop translated the Miraculous Image of Our Lady from the old wooden church into the new one, thereby acknowledging the apparitions and the cult of the Holy Image. The saintly cowherd Mikołaj, who had been released from prison during the epidemic and had continued to lead a modest and quiet life, did not live to

M arian Chapel of the Immaculate Conception

see this great and joyous day of glory. He regretted that there was no church or chapel in Grąblin Wood, in the holy place where Mary had walked. He prophesied that there would come a time when a beautiful church would be built there in Mary's honour, and that if people did not do this, then angels would accomplish the task.

When this is going to happen, we do not yet know, but I am sure that the grateful people will one day put up a church there for their Queen.

The cowherd fasted much and did penance. He never parted with his rosary, which he wore around his neck. Although he was accorded universal respect, he never put himself above other people. He foretold the day and hour of his death. Although he felt absolutely healthy, he called a priest, received the last sacraments and died on 23rd April 1857 *in odore sanctitatis*. He was buried in a wooden coffin in the old churchyard at Licheń. 40 years later, when a new monument was being put up, his grave and coffin were opened and the visionary's body was found intact. In 1948 a small statue of the Immaculate Conception was put on Mikołaj's grave. On 4th May 1975, on the 125th anniversary of the apparitions, a splendid mausoleum for this man of heaven was unveiled. A tomb was placed over his grave, with the figures of Our Lady, the cowherd, and the pine-tree picturing one of the apparitions next to it on a small elevation. In the village of Grąblin a little chapel stands on the spot where Mikołaj's house was once situated. Devout people believe he is a saint and come to pray at his graveside, bring flowers and light candles, and ask for his intercession with God.

FOUNT OF GRACE

The cult of Our Lady of Licheń, which began during the epidemic, grew and quickly spread throughout Central Poland. Although in the old days the road to Licheń was tiring, and on the spot there were no special facilities for pilgrims, not even any drinking water, every year tens of thousands of people came for the anniversary of the apparitions, for the Feast of the Assumption. 86 parishes would come with processions. In the days when Poland was not independent people would come here to pray for their country's freedom. Sinners would come to confess their sins and do penance for the sins they had committed. People who needed assistance also came, to beseech Mary in matters where there was no hope. Parents would bring their children. There is a belief that Our Lady of Licheń has special blessings for children and young people. In Licheń Graveyard youngsters would be shown the common grave of the Insurgents of 1863, to instil a sense of patriotism and self-sacrifice in them.

The holy place was full of spiritual life, and its external aspects also thrived. The beautiful park founded by Father Kosiński was the ornament of the hillside. In 1871 Count Kwilecki founded a church organ. Other benefactors purchased vestments and liturgical vessels, carpets, banners, and pictures for the church.

In 1872 the new parish priest, Father Jankowski, extended the church by adding a new chancel; and the parish priest in 1903, Father Stanisław Maniewski, renewed the two sacristies and a small chapel, and put up a brick wall to protect the pine-tree in Grąblin Wood. During the First World War Licheń managed to escape serious damage. The Prussians removed three bells from the bell-tower and some tin organ-pipes from the organ. In the academic year of 1921/22 a young seminarian from Włocławek, Stefan Wyszyński, who was later to become Primate of Poland, was staying at Licheń on a period of rest to improve his health (he was running the risk of contracting tuberculosis).

THE DARK NIGHT OF WAR

The Second World War broke out. Poland was the first country to be invaded by the Nazis. On the part of Poland annexed directly onto the Third Reich the Nazis launched a gruesome offensive campaign against the Catholic Church, its clergy and its churches. They knew that they would never manage to break the Polish nation's spirit until they subdued the Church and crushed the faith.

The Holy Shrine of Licheń was one of the victims of this barbarity. On 24th August 1940 Licheń's parish priest, Father Jan Przydacz, was arrested and deported to the concentration camp at Dachau. The Nazis decided to turn the church and presbytery into a Hitlerjugend training camp. The altars and church furnishings were hacked down and burned. The vestments were stolen. The helm on the church tower was pulled down, the fences were removed, the memorials were demolished, shots were fired at the crosses, and statues of Our Lady were smashed.

There is a surviving miraculous image of Jesus on the Cross at which Bertha Bauer, a political propaganda instructor, took shots.

The Marian Fathers' house, view of the west elevation

*T*he Holy Father with 200 Marian Fathers, Licheń, June 7th, 1999

God's retribution soon reached the desecrator. She was shot dead just a few hours after having committed the profanation. Another extant piece found later was the head of a statue of Our Lady, which was hacked with an axe by a traitor and collaborator, Stefan Marciniak. The same man, who claimed *Volksdeutsch* ("local German") status, also gave orders for the cross on the church tower to be broken up and thrown into a dunghill. He came to a miserable end, too.

In the Hitlerjugend camp a group of 180 boys between the ages of 16 and 18 were trained in brutality and crime. One of the items on their syllabus was a pogrom staged by these young people on the Polish inhabitants of the surrounding villages. All of them — old people, women, children, and infants — were beaten. People were tortured for no reason at all. Another item in the training scheme was the torture and murder of young Polish men and women. Half of the inhabitants of the parish were evicted from their homes.

In January 1945 the Nazis rounded up a large group of men and told them to dig a huge mass grave near the church. There was an order for the entire parish to be murdered. However the people of Licheń and its neighbourhood were saved by a rapid offensive by the liberation forces. On the 30th anniversary of liberation a tall memorial cross was put up in gratitude.

The losses the shrine had incurred were colossal. All that was left after the wartime destruction were the four walls of the church and the Holy Image, which was saved by a miracle. In the autumn of 1940 Nazi policemen were sent from Gosławice for the Image. In spite of their desperate attempts, they could not manage to wrest open the enclosure in which the Image was kept. They forced the church organist, Bolesław Lisowski, to open it for them, threatening him with violence. But he could not pull up the blind, which was not heavy and affixed to a beam, either. Suddenly, while they were struggling, shouts were heard from the village. The policemen ran out of the church to see what was going on. When they were gone the organist pulled up the blind with no difficulty at all, removed the Miraculous Image, hid it behind a side-altar, and put another picture in its place. The blind gently slid down again. It turned out that all was quiet in the village and nothing had happened. The Nazis returned to the church and now had no problems with opening up the enclosure, but the image they were looking for was no longer there.

The Nazis locked up the church and took the keys to their station at Gosławice. A few nights later three parishioners, Bolesław Lisowski the organist, Stanisław Gorczewski the churchwarden, and a Racinowski, got into the church through a window, removed the Miraculous Image and hid it for safe keeping in a private house.

When the occupying authorities later returned to the matter and set up an investigation in search of the picture of the Madonna, it was taken away to Maliniec and hidden in a manor house which was managed by a steward named Kietliński.

In March 1945 the Miraculous Image of Our Lady returned to Licheń from Maliniec and put in the organist's house. The local people tidied up and decorated the church as best they could. On a Sunday in March Father Konstanty Hytry, parish priest of Gosławice, led a procession for the translation of the picture to the church, and then celebrated Mass. Mary had returned to Her children.

The Diocese of Włocławek suffered huge losses during the War. Many churches had been completely destroyed by the Nazis. Over 220 diocesan priests, including Bishop Michał Kozal, had died martyr's deaths in the prisons and concentration camps. Others who survived now returned to the diocese, but with their health ruined and a shorter life expectancy. Many parishes had no priest at all. The church authorities at Włocławek appealed to priests from other dioceses to come and work in the vacant parishes.

One of the priests who responded was Father Aleksander Dobrucki from Volhynia (now beyond Poland's current eastern border), who became parish priest at Licheń.

The Congregation of the Marian Fathers also came to work in the Diocese of Włocławek, and was allocated the Parish of Pyzdry.

THE MARIAN FATHERS AT LICHEŃ

By the 17th century, when Poland had been a Christian and Catholic country for nearly seven centuries already, there were hundreds of religious houses, both contemplative and apostolic, throughout the land. All the nations of Europe had produced great founders of religious orders, which had come to Poland and established their houses in that country. But up to that time no Polish man had endeavoured to set up a new, specifically Polish order. The Venerable Servant of God Father Stanisław Papczyński was the first Pole to undertake the task. He was born at Podegrodzie near Stary Sącz in southern Poland. In 1673 he founded a new, Polish order, called the Order of the Marian Fathers of the

Immaculate Conception of the Blessed Virgin Mary. The Marian Fathers could thus be said to have grown up out of the cult of the Virgin Mary which is part of the spirit of the Polish nation, and on Polish soil. One would therefore have expected that they should enjoy the support and affection of the Polish people, and the assistance of the local bishops. Alas, it has not been like that. We Poles have always preferred what is from abroad to our own. We are impressed by foreign ideas and foreign goods, and even the Western way of life. This attitude has also had its effect on the history and development of the new Order.

From the very outset the Marian Fathers have never had an easy life. Founded by a peasant's son, they have never been a wealthy order nor enjoyed the patronage of influential persons. They worked in villages with the poorest inhabitants, and along with them suffered hardship. As they were a Polish order, they met with particularly severe forms of oppression at the hands of the partitioning powers when Poland lost its independence. Many of the Order's most outstanding members died in the national uprisings, in prison or in exile.

In 1864 the Tsar issued a decree closing down the Order. It was disbanded and some of its members were arrested. The most re-solute were sent to a monastery at Mariampol in Lithuania, where they were to remain until they died.

By 1909 there was only one Marian Father still left in the house at Mariampol, Father Wincenty Senkowski, the Order's General. Risking his life, he secretly renewed the Order, receiving into it Father Jerzy Matulewicz (Matulaitis) and Father Franciszek Buczys. The Order was saved and began to grow again. Unfor-tunately another blow came with the Second World War.

In 1954 the Order's mother house and seminary at Bielany, Warsaw, were closed down. Very hard times started for the community. Satan was wreaking his vengeance on an Order which was proud of its name after the Virgin Mary and which had a special reverence for this Patron.

The Miraculous Image of Our Lady of Licheń with the Pontifical Crown

◄ ───

In 1948, when the Marian Fathers were working at Pyzdry, a former member of the Order, Father Franciszek Korszyński, was Bishop of Włocławek. It was his wish that his fellows from the community should assume the responsibilities for the Shrine at Licheń. He lodged an application with this request to the Provincial Board of the Marian Fathers in Warsaw. Although there were no members of the community readily available, the Bishop was insistent and we had to assume the work at Licheń. Our preliminary visitation nearly turned into a tragedy. Satan evidently did not want Mary's Shrine at Licheń to be placed in the care of Her spiritual sons. It was October 1948. I was a novice in the Order's house at Skurc near Siedlce. Once day Father Provincial Władysław Łysik visited us and told us the following story about his expedition to Licheń.

Towards the end of September Father Provincial and his Deputy, Father Władysław Lewandowski, set out from Warsaw on a visitation of Licheń, as suggested by the Bishop. Their journey to Konin took several hours. From Konin they travelled on a narrow-gauge railway to Gosławice. The sun was already starting to set when they alighted from this slow train. They were shown a narrow path winding amid the lakes, bushes and marshes. They had walked a few miles when night fell. They had no torch with them. For several miles here were no villages, and not a soul in sight.

They went on their way groping in the dark, when suddenly they felt that they had stumbled into a marsh and were sinking. Both Fathers were quite stout and dressed in cassocks with briefcases in their hands. They started calling out for help, but out in the wilderness no-one could hear them. They held hands, and this made them sink even deeper into the quagmire. In a short while they would both go down and no-one would ever find out what had happened to them. In a desperate plight, they started calling on Our Lady of Licheń for help, for it was to Her that their journey was taking them.

And suddenly in the dark Father Provincial Łysik caught hold of a drooping bough of a tree. He got a firm grip and slowly both priests managed to stagger out onto a little island in the middle of the marsh. Wet and cold, they stayed on the island to daybreak, thanking God for their delivery. When the sun rose they went on their way, and wandering over the marshes and wasteland they finally reached a settlement, but it was Grąblin, not Licheń. They were covered with mud from head to foot and totally exhausted. The villagers provided them with assistance, helping them wash and clean their clothes, giving them a meal and showing the road to Licheń.

Father Provincial told us novices that he had never in his life seen such a poor village. Everywhere the soil was sandy, and there were forests, quagmires, and lakes. The tiny cottages were built of mud and had wattle roofs. The church on the sandy hill was quite empty; it had been pillaged by the Nazis. The Miraculous Image was quite small, and it was hanging on the wall of the chancel. Next to the exiguous presbytery there was just an old byre. They visited all of these buildings, but did not say Mass, for when the local parish priest learned what the reason was for their visit he was very displeased and did not let them approach the altar. They returned 16 kilometres (10 miles) on foot to Konin Station, with very mixed feelings. They determined that the Marian Fathers would not come here, in spite of the Bishop's insistence. That was when I first heard of Licheń and its tiny image of the Blessed Virgin. My young heart could not as yet anticipate the huge work that it would have to undertake at Licheń in the spreading abroad in and beyond Poland of the fame of Our Lady of Licheń.

Meanwhile Father Provincial and his Deputy were on the train back to Warsaw, extremely fatigued and with an ever firmer determination that the Marian Fathers would not come to Licheń. But Our Lady had quite different plans. In spite of the difficulties and the reluctance of Father Dobrucki and the people of Licheń, who cast abuse at Dean Perliński and the priests who arrived with him, eventually chasing them out, on 23rd April 1949 the Marian Fathers eventually assumed the responsibilities for the Parish and Shrine of Licheń.

Pontifical coronation ceremony of Our Lady of Licheń, 15th August, 1967

After a symbolic figure of 99 years Mary's prophecy was fulfilled that a monastery would be established at Licheń, and that Her sons would be the guardians of Her image. She seems to have seen to it Herself that the promise should be kept within the century. The first years were extremely difficult. The Congregation had no additional material or human resources to man the sanctuary and supervise its development. Moreover the times were not auspicious at all for growth. The first parish priest of Licheń under the Marian Fathers was Father Henryk Tomaszewski. He was followed by Father Józef Glinka, who held the office for 7 years. The Marian Congregation had to start everything from scratch. The presbytery and the church (except for the tiny Miraculous Image on the chancel wall) were empty, and there were no out-buildings in the farm. There were no altars, church furnishings, vessels or vestments. The local people fed the priests, who were destitute. Since the Parish of Licheń has always been

Monument of Cardinal Stefan Wyszyński, Primate of Poland

✱ 1901 — † 1981

M

„WSZYSTKO POSTAWIŁEM NA MARYJE."
ŚWIETLANEJ PAMIĘCI KSIĘDZA KARDYNAŁA STEFANA WYSZYŃSKIEGO
KORONATORA WIZERUNKU LICHEŃSKIEJ MADONNY,
KTÓRY JAKO ALUMN SEMINARIUM WE WŁOCŁAWKU W LATACH 1922 - 1923
W LICHENIU NA PLEBANII MIESZKAŁ, UCZYŁ DZIECI RELIGII
I MODLIŁ SIĘ PRZED CUDOWNYM OBRAZEM O ŻYCIE, ZDROWIE I KAPŁAŃSTWO.
ZA PRZYCZYNĄ MARYI - BOLESNEJ KRÓLOWEJ POLSKI
ZOSTAŁ WYSŁUCHANY. ZE ŚMIERTELNEJ CHOROBY UZDROWIONY,
KAPŁAŃSTWEM I BISKUPSTWEM OBDAROWANY,
PRZEZ BOGA DANY POLSKIEMU NARODOWI - JAKO PRYMAS TYSIĄCLECIA,
STAŁ SIĘ DUCHOWYM OJCEM PAPIEŻA POLAKA JANA PAWŁA II.

POMNIK WYSTAWIŁA DUCHOWA RODZINA MARIAŃSKA
R. P. 1982

very small and the people impoverished, years passed and the wartime losses could not be made up for. However the cult was growing. The people who had suffered much during the War came to Our Lady for consolation. The pilgrimages started anew.

1952 marked the centenary anniversary of the Holy Image's translation from the forest to Licheń. The preparations for the celebrations were carried out in extremely difficult conditions. The times were very hard, but in spite of this tens of thousands came for the Jubilee on August 15th.

A huge area amid the gorse was made ready for the ceremony. There were hundreds of church banners fluttering in the wind. The procession which followed the same route as the translation a hundred years earlier from the spot where Our Lady had appeared to Licheń Hill stretched for 2 kilometres. It was a gigantic demonstration of faith and veneration of the Blessed Virgin. Unfortunately the following year there were no more auxiliary processions from the neighbouring parishes for the Feast, and over the next years pilgrims came only privately, as individuals. The development scheme for the Shrine could not be started, either.

SACRUM POLONIAE MILLENNIUM

1966, the millennial anniversary of Poland's receiving Christianity, was ahead. The Bishops of Poland took a decision that part of the Jubilee celebrations would be a tribute of gratitude paid to the Blessed Virgin Mary. A resolution was passed that in each of the dioceses there would be a coronation ceremony for one of the miraculous images of Our Lady.

In the ancient Diocese of Włocławek there are 25 such miraculous images. Some are many centuries old, look splendid, are housed in magnificent churches, and receive a lot of veneration. Bishop Antoni Pawłowski, head of the diocese, appointed a special commission consisting of several senior clergymen. The commission was to visit all the shrines of Our Lady within the diocese so that it could then put forward a recommendation to the deans and chapters which of them to select for the diocesan coronation.

On its itinerary the Commission missed Licheń, in the belief that this image had no chance to be accorded a pontifical crown. Its location was very awkward, 16 kilometres away on a sandy road from the nearest railway station. The church was small and empty. It needed a general restoration, conversion and decoration. The premises had no facilities, not even a perimeter fence, and the holy image itself was tiny and somewhat worn. The hard times had made the cult of Our Lady of Licheń decline somewhat.

The fact that it was Our Lady of Licheń Who received the Pontifical Crown during the Millennial Jubilee is Her own doing and secret. This is what Bishop Kazimierz Majdański, who was Chairman of the Licheń Coronation Committee, said publicly after the coronation ceremony.

Father Leon Szeląg, Provincial of the Marian Fathers, entrusted a member of the Order, Father Eugeniusz Makulski, who held a master's degree in History, with the preparation of the historical records and documents, other business connected with the application for the granting of a pontifical crown, and the preparations in the shrine itself and of the ceremony.

There was not too much time, and the task was challenging and responsible. An arduous inquiry needed to be carried out in the archives and libraries, both church and secular. The collection and recording of the testimonials for the vast local tradition used up a lot of the time. Although much of the documentation had been lost in outcome of the Second World War it turned out that what had managed to survive was still a daunting amount, extremely interesting, but had received very little attention before. In the light of the source materials which were discovered the apparitions and the Shrine itself acquired a new vigour. Finally all the exhausting work involved was successfully accomplished. In November 1965, on examining the applications and evidence, the Holy Father Pope Paul VI and the Vatican Chapter issued and

*A*ll year round Our Lady of Licheń welcomes pilgrims and visitors at Her Shrine

publicly announced a decree which said that he thereby recognised the Picture of Our Lady of Licheń, Sorrowful Queen of Poland, which was renowned for the graces bestowed through it, as a Miraculous Image and recommended the conferring of a Pontifical Crown upon it on his behalf.

In November 1965, too, a special farewell ceremony was held at Licheń and the image was dispatched to Warsaw for renovation and conservation. There a group of specialists conducted an official procedure removing the silver robe from the painting in which Our Lady had been enrobed in 1864, after the fall of the November Uprising against the Russian partitioning power, to cover up the national emblems (the Eagle and the inscription). Next the painting was submitted to a thorough process of renovation and dressed in a new metallic superficial robe and crown. The entire image was put into a sumptuous new frame. Eight more golden eagles on silver escutcheons, for the times since the Piast dynasty in the Middle Ages up to the present day, keep vigil at the side of their Queen. The upper part of the frame bears the arms of the Pope, the Primate of Poland, the Marian Fathers, and Licheń. The lower part carries the dates of 966 and 1966, for the Baptism of Poland and its Millennial Jubilee, along with an inscription in Polish meaning "Poland is ever faithful." The background of the image is laid with royal purple. A space was left at the top in the background over the image of the Virgin for the Pontifical Crown.

The conservation work on the miraculous image was conducted by a conservation specialist, Ada Popławska. The artist Wacław Markowski made the metal robe and crown which overlies the image. The new lime-wood frame was designed by Father Eugeniusz Makulski and made by the sculptor Stefan Wędołowski. Antoni Górakiewicz applied the surface layer of gold leaf. By the end of June 1966 all the work had been completed. On July 3rd and 4th the miraculous image was put on display in the Church of Our Lady of Lourdes in Warsaw. Huge crowds of Varsovians come in procession to the Holy Image to pay their respects to our

Queen. There were several miraculous cures. Mary showered graces bountifully on the faithful inhabitants of Poland's capital city, and then She returned home to Licheń.

HER THIRD RETURN

A chronicle records the welcome given the Mother of God on Her return to Licheń in the following way. It was Saturday, July 30th, 1966. It was a beautiful, warm and sunny day, fragrant with the harvest and the perfume of summer flowers. At six o'clock in the evening the bell from the church tower started tolling a welcome. A huge crowd had gathered. At half past six a procession left the church and headed for the presbytery. The priests robed in vestments carried the renovated Miraculous Image onto the porch and showed it to the people. A fanfare sounded an anthem of welcome. The crowd was deeply moved: they could see Mary in all Her splendour, with the White Eagle on Her Immaculate Heart and with a crown on Her head. After 102 years of concealment, they could again see the image of Our Lady of Licheń just as it really is. There was no longer a sad gown betokening enthralment covering it. After the fanfare had been sounded the image was placed on its throne and put on the small altar which had been set up in front of the church door. Here the parish priest, Father Eugeniusz Makulski, promoter of the cult, the parents, children, young people, altar-servers and flower-girls of the Parish, welcomed Our Lady. The choir sang a hymn of welcome, and then the fanfare sounded again, while in solemn procession the priests carried the Miraculous Image into the Church of Our Lady of Częstochowa. A vigil of prayer and services interspersed with preaching lasted the whole night. Confessions were heard and the Sorrowful Queen of Poland was paid a joyous tribute of devotion.

From five o'clock in the morning of Sunday, July 31st 1966 until eleven the same morning a series of masses, one after another, was said in front of the Miraculous Image. At eleven the clergy and congregation in a long procession followed the long route from the small church to the new brick-built church, to transfer the Image there. In compliance with the ancient custom, the Image was carried by parties of priests, who changed at regular intervals. When the Image had been set up over the high altar, Father Makulski read out an announcement about some of the most recent reports of graces received thanks to the intercession of Our Lady of Licheń. Next he uncovered and blessed 22 display cabinets full of votive offerings. After this, again to the sound of a fanfare, the curtain over the Miraculous Image which had been put into a wooden casing inlaid with a purple cloth, was solemnly drawn back. The congregation which had flocked to attend this historic ceremony wept with emotion. The Holy Image was so beautiful.

I was honoured to be able to celebrate Mass at this unforgettable moment in time, for the intentions of the artists and benefactors, my family and friends, and all those who had helped me to accomplish the task of fully renovating the Holy Image.

O, Mary, be praised and accept this humble effort in token of my filial affection and love for You. May this joyous day be an encouragement and the hope that even extremely difficult matters undertaken for the glory of God and in honour of His Immaculate Mother may be successfully achieved.

The ceremony was concluded with the patriotic anthem *Boże coś Polskę,* a deeply meaningful act before the Sorrowful Queen of Poland in Her Miraculous Image. On 15th August 1966 the celebrations for the Feast of the Assumption were held as usual in Licheń, but this time in conjunction with the festivities for the Millennium of Poland's Baptism. The year of preparation in the Diocese of Włocławek for the coronation ceremony started, under the presiding auspices of Bishop Kazimierz Majdański.

On 22nd December 1966 Bishop Antoni Pawłowski, head of the Diocese of Włocławek, appointed Father Makulski parish priest of Licheń and custodian of Our Lady's Shrine.

*I*nterior of St. Dorothy's Church

Main altar, St. Dorothy's Church, with the Miraculous Image over it

THE PONTIFICAL CROWN

On 15th August, 1967, all the Bishops of Poland and around 150 thousand pilgrims from the entire country came to Licheń. 47 thousand people received the Blessed Sacrament. There were 480 priests and monks, and over 250 nuns in attendance. There were four celebrants who performed the coronation ceremony: Cardinal Stefan Wyszyński, Primate of Poland; Bishop Antoni Pawłowski of Włocławek; Archbishop Antoni Baraniak of Poznań; and Bishop Wilhelm Pluta of Gorzów. Our Lady's prophetic words spoken to the cowherd Mikołaj, that the entire Polish nation would come to this image and draw strength from Her hands, came true.

In a marvellous sermon, Cardinal Wyszyński said:

"When we look at the countenance of Our Blessed Lady enthroned at Licheń Church, we see the White Eagle, emblem of our native land on Earth, on Her bosom. Let's not be surprised at this! Did not Mary sing of Herself, *Henceforth all nations shall call Me blessed*, whereby She meant the Polish Nation as well. Therefore She clasps the White Eagle unto Her bosom, in token of Her motherhood to our Country. This emblem was prosecuted in the times of our enthralment. It vexed our invaders, the enemies of God and our Country, and for this reason had to remain hidden beneath a silver robe. Is this not meaningful?"

"The emblem of our Country was safe on the bosom which nursed the Saviour of the World. May this bond between the Mother of God and our Country mark out a path for us to follow; may it constantly remind us of the covenant which the Polish nation has entered with Mary. May it constantly show us where we are to seek assistance and support in adversity and danger."

In this sermon the Primate said that in 1920-22, when he was a seminary priest in Włocławek, he spent some time at Licheń to recuperate his health. He was suffering from severe tuberculosis, and his condition was so bad that he no longer had any hopes of either graduating from the seminary or of being ordained, or indeed of living for much longer. Everyone was convinced that his days had been numbered. It was in such a grave condition that Father Ignacy Rudziński, parish priest at Licheń, brought him there. "I begged Our Lady of Licheń to give me the strength just sufficient for ordination and so that I could say just one Mass. I would not have minded dying immediately after that Mass. But Mary gave me much more than I asked for; She gave me so much that here I am today, after 45 years I have returned to Licheń to put this crown on the Holy Father's behalf on Her sacred brow."

So Poland owes it to Our Lady of Licheń that at the turn of our millennia of Christianity She gave us a great spiritual leader, our Primate Cardinal Stefan Wyszyński.

***

After the coronation ceremony Bishop Antoni Pawłowski of Włocławek issued a declaration that Our Lady of Licheń was the Patron of the Konin and Turek Basin, of miners, metallurgists, transport workers, and those employed in the power industries; and that She was the patron of the entire working class.

Another prophecy was fulfilled: Mary's words when She said to Mikołaj the cowherd that straight roads would be built in the area. When the cowherd told people about this they laughed at him asking him who would ever build roads through the forests, lakes, moors and marshes. No-one could have had the slightest suspicion then that the area of Konin was rich in subterranean mineral resources and that within the space of a century a mighty forest of steel electricity pylons, along with the chimneys of steelworks and a power station would shoot up into the sky in the locality, giving jobs for thousands.

But man does not live by bread alone, but by the grace and word of God... Those straight roads which Mary had foretold were a preview of our own days. And in foreseeing the laboriousness of those times, She also made ready for her people, who would be

Licheń's outdoor Golgotha

exhausted by work, an oasis of spiritual life, a fount of grace, a repast for the human soul.

No wonder that the hard-working people of the Basin have so deep an affection and love for their Patron, and visit Her in such large numbers. Every year on the Sunday following August 15th there are special services here for industrial workers.

The people of Konin and its neighbourhood sincerely love Licheń, which is sometimes called the New Częstochowa or the Częstochowa of Northern Poland. They regard the Miraculous Image of Licheń as their most precious treasure. They spend whole days and nights here praying before the Holy Countenance, and here they are endowed with profound spiritual experiences and numerous graces which the Sorrowful Queen of Poland generously showers on all who seek Her intercession.

Polish men and women from all the other parts of Poland, and indeed from abroad as well, hold this Image in just as deep a reverence. It was Mary Herself, when she came to Earth to visit Polish soil, discovered this patriotic image of Herself in a woodland shrine, blessed it and chose it for the sign of Her great love for the Polish Nation. She singled out this Image as a mighty fount of special grace for the suffering people. She Herself wished to be venerated in this Image by all Polish hearts, wherever they may be, whether in Poland or abroad.

There will come a time when every Polish family will keep this Holy Image in a place of honour, for it is the Nation's signpost into its second millennium, on the road initiated by the vows made to Mary in the first millennium. This Image expresses the profound meaning in Catholic Poland's self-subjection to the Blessed Virgin's will. Just as following defeat at Leipzig Poland's White Eagle found a safe haven in the care of the Mother of God, so today every Polish man and woman, every Polish family, the entire country, may find a safe haven in the heart of Poland's Ever-Victorious Queen.

There will come a time when millions of Polish people shall wear the medal of the Sorrowful Queen of Poland round their necks. Millions will carry Her picture in their purses or pockets, a symbol that they belong to the Polish Nation and that they are faithful to Mary. There will come a time when many churches will be erected throughout the land in honour of the Sorrowful Queen of Poland. There will come a time when every village throughout Poland will set up a wayside shrine in its midst and invite the Sorrowful Queen to dwell among its inhabitants. Artists and painters will find it hard to keep pace with the innumerable commissions they will receive for this Image; there will be so many people wishing to have a copy. There will be so many ceremonial introductions and welcomes for the Sorrowful Queen.

She will descend from Licheń Hill and pervade the entire country, to take all the towns and cities, the hamlets and the villages, and the families into her safe-keeping. Already during the apparitions Mary promised that She would save and comfort all who pray before this Image of Hers. The Mother of God keeps Her word: She will save that person, that family, that village and city in which people invite Her into their homes and entrust their hearts to Her. Today's times are by no means easy for the Family of Man. Let us call upon the Mother of the Church in the words of the prayer on the Licheń Image: "O, Queen of Poland, grant peace to our days!" Today it is that prayer for the great gift of peace that is the need of the times. The Queen of Peace has the power to grant us the grace of peace.

Just as years ago the translation of the Image marked the beginning of the Shrine's history, so the coronation began a new chapter in that story. Not only was the Shrine with its entire grounds thoroughly redecorated, but many new graces and miracles came from Mary's maternal and regal hands, for thousands of people. The numerous cures and other graces obtained are attracting pilgrims to Licheń from all over Poland, and now every Sunday is celebrated here like a major feast-day. There are also pilgrims from abroad, especially expatriate Poles visiting their home country. News and information about Poland's Lourdes is translated into many languages and published in various religious magazines and periodicals outside Poland.

M odel of Licheń Basilica

***

Dear Reader, I have now told you the story, although in a brief outline, of the apparitions of Our Lady at Licheń and the history of the Shrine itself. I am sure there are still many questions you would like to ask. No doubt you would like me to describe the extraordinary graces and miracles that people have experienced here, but unfortunately there is no room for that in this little booklet. However I would like to add that there are many extraordinary and amazing things about all the events connected with this tremendous gift from Heaven.

First there are the apparitions themselves. Our Lady appeared not to monks, not to children, nor to a pure maiden, but to two grown men. One was a soldier wounded in battle, and the second a cowherd in a woodland wilderness.

There were no other people during the apparitions. Our Lady did not announce Her return earlier; She did not establish a venue. She appeared in different places each time; on one occasion it was in the cowherd's simple cottage at Grąblin.

She appeared unexpectedly. On three occasions there were other persons present during the vision; they observed the cowherd's strange behaviour, but could not understand it and did not see anything else.

The miracles that were visible to others were the cowherd's sudden rejuvenation and the light and lightning on the day of the image's translation. This was to be Heaven's verification of all that Mikołaj had said.

The Miraculous Image is also extraordinary in that within its diminutive dimensions it expresses a momentous message — both in the religious and in the national, Polish sense.

**

Our kind, understanding and very loving Mother lives at Licheń. She is not awesome in Her power, not overwhelming in Her majesty, not bedazzling with riches. She looks down gently with Her eyes half-closed, listening to the words of all Her children.

Whoever should see this Image just once in his life shall never forget it. Whoever should come to this hill just once and kneel in this church shall never forget this place. In his heart and mind he will return here time and again; he will be longing for it.

***

Dear venerators of the Blessed Virgin, I have told you the story of the Shrine of the Sorrowful Queen of Poland not only to satisfy your curiosity, but also to encourage you to improve your lives and to do penance. Who of us can say that he is without sin, that he has never in his life offended God or made his beloved Mother sad? So if there has been sin and transgression, there must be penance, amendment, and prayer, for it is a terrible thing to fall into the hands of a wrathful God. We should be doing penance for the sins committed in Poland and in the whole world. There are so many sins being committed, and they are so terrible!

Let us listen to the beseeching words of Our Lady of Licheń, "Mary, Sorrowful Queen of Poland." Should we not stop and think about that name and appellation? Why is She "sorrowful"? Because the Polish Nation, which She loves so deeply and on which She has lavished so much of Her loving care, which She

*T*he Holy Trinity Chapel in the Basilica

*C*hapel of the 108 Martyrs in the Basilica

has defended for a thousand years — today pays such little heed to the Divine Mercy and is committing sins that cry out to Heaven for vengeance.

God's commandments are being trampled underfoot; God's laws are being infringed. The blood of countless unborn children is being shed; hearts are being depraved by impurity and hatred. Who shall help us wrest ourselves free of our dreadful addictions, habits and sins? Who shall revive us spiritually? Who shall vanquish Satan and liberate us from his power? Let us turn our eyes to Our Lady!

I speak about this to you, beloved brothers and sisters, to encourage you to trustfully pray to Our Lady. Who of you does not have his worries and cares? Who of you does not have his own bitter cup to drink, his own cross to bear? Who does not have a family tragedy, physical or spiritual? Perhaps, if you are a wife, you are watching the marital love between you quickly die, and your family's happiness crumbling about you. Perhaps, if you are a mother, you are watching the child which you so lovingly nursed and brought up waiting for you to die. You taught that child his prayers as he sat on your lap; you took him to Mass and to Holy Communion, but now he has forsaken God for an evil woman, he has sold his soul to the devil, he is dazed and heading for eternal damnation.

Perhaps you are in tears, sitting at the bedside of someone who is dying and you are watching all that is the essence of your own life being drained away. The tragedy is just a few steps away, and there is nowhere you can turn to for help.

Perhaps on sleepless nights terrible memories of the sins of your childhood, youth, or mature years haunt you. Sins of impurity that you committed when you were young, the wrong done to a young woman, the tears in a mother's eyes, whom you hurt, the work-wearied hands of your father, whom you did not help. Or perhaps you can hear the crying of that baby you did not allow to be born!

After many years the ghosts of those for who we were the cause of corruption or ruin return to haunt us.

Perhaps your creditors or those you have wronged keep returning. Perhaps the pangs of conscience are caused by a betrayed wife's tears, or the tears of those children who suffered because of your drunkenness. So many years have passed, but maybe you cannot get that perjured confession and sacrilegious Communion out of your mind. You are terrified when you think of yourself standing before the Judgement Throne. Who will then save you from eternal damnation? Who will obtain God's Mercy for you? Mary — the Refuge of the greatest sinners in the world!

At times of worry, at those bitter moments that life brings us every day, who will comfort us and bring us help, to whom can we confide our sorrows and our suffering, and our loneliness? On whose shoulder can we cry, to whom can we open up our hearts?

Only to the Sorrowful Mother, who understands human suffering and human anxiety because She is the Sorrowful Mother. Let us in confidence beg for Her intercession, for today, as She stands beside God's throne in Her role of Interceder of grace, She wishes and is able to come to our aid and consolation.

Let us not forget about the gratitude which we owe Mary, either. Who of us may say that he has never been heard out by Mary, that She has never comforted and strengthened him, that he has absolutely nothing to thank her for?

Let us take a look at our own lives: perhaps that moment of assistance came during the War, or perhaps it was by during the funeral of a near and dear person, or at life's crossroads, or on the sickbed, when the doctors had given us up as a hopeless case, perhaps in the loneliness and desolation of orphanhood or old age, or imprisonment, or even facing the firing-squad, or in exile in a foreign land...

To whom did we then turn with our complaints? Whose name did those livid lips utter? Whose image did those frightened eyes seek? Who was it who really helped us then, who bent over us, took us by the hand, consoled our faint heart?

MARY! MARY! MARY!

Let us review our lives. As the night sky is spangled with stars, so too our lives are full of the graces so generously bestowed by the Blessed Virgin. And how do we thank Her for it? Have we kept our promises, have we conducted the pilgrimages, have we carried out the spiritual vows we made? Let's not forget: there will still come a moment in the life of each one of us when we shall be yet again calling on Mary and asking for Her intercession.

Remember — any time you need Her, She will come to you with comfort and help. Pray to Her sincerely, commend yourself and your nearest and dearest to Her. Invite Her into your house, even if it is only in the form of a small picture. Become Her champion, Her faithful, loving child.

*P*laques commemorating benefactors on Founders' Wall

***

Since the coronation the Shrine at Licheń is gradually emerging from its wartime devastation and is becoming more and more beautiful every day thanks to the tremendous effort being made by its parishioners, pilgrims, and members of the Marian Family. It is offering facilities for more and more pilgrims, and is all the time becoming better appointed for the worship of God. Our congregations love Our Lady and they are helping as much as they can in our development project. Those who know Licheń from the past and who see it now are amazed how much the joyous love of Mary can accomplish. The faithful and loving people of Poland wish to provide their Mother and Queen with a fitting house. There has never been a want of generous hearts among them for a blessed cause. The churches raised by our forefathers are memorials to their deep faith, the nation's most

precious treasures. Today there is no dearth of generous persons in
Poland, either. All the churches which were destroyed during the
Second World War have been splendidly restored, just as the rest
of the country has been rebuilt, too. Today in Licheń what is most
needed is a large church.

On 19th September 1965, as I was travelling in a car to take up
permanent residence at Licheń, two kilometres before the Shrine
a vision of a beautiful basilica with fine white walls flashed
through my imagination. I could see its many towers topped with
golden crowns sparkling in the sunlight. Over the years of my
work in Licheń I dreamed of such a spacious church, and prayed
I would be able to start the work for it.

The thought of La Salette comes to my mind, and the huge
basilica and facilities for pilgrims that were constructed on
a mountain-top in the Alps. What trouble those people must have
gone to building in those conditions! I think of Lourdes. Three
mighty basilicas have been erected there, and an entire city to
serve the pilgrims. The Portuguese nation has raised a basilica in

Chapel of the Blessed Honoratus

the small village of Fatima, along with all the infrastructure the pilgrims need. Not so long ago, within our memories, Our Lady wept in a plaster image at Syracuse, Italy. Now on the spot where not so long ago there was a working-class house there is a fine basilica and a huge place of pilgrimage. How does Poland's Licheń, the place of such stupendous apparitions and such marvellous spiritual and physical graces, compare? At Lourdes and Fatima Our Lady asked for a chapel to be built for the cult, and people erected magnificent basilicas. At Licheń She asked for a church, and even added that if that church were not built She would send angels from heaven to perform the task. Evidently the Mother of God very much wanted a large church to serve as a sanctuary for the pilgrims once they reached the place, after a good deal of hardship in getting there. But the Polish nation could not undertake such a building project, since it had foreign masters and no freedom to exercise its will. The two decades between the World Wars were hardly enough for such a task. Then after the Second World War came another period of slavery that continued for so many years.

Today, when freedom has finally come, society is split up spiritually and for many who are fighting for survival times are hard. So we have no fine works of art, famous paintings, alabaster sculptures, or treasury with souvenirs and heirlooms. But we can do without them. What we desperately need is a big new church. We already have two fine churches, but they are tiny. We have a number of chapels, but they only cater for individual groups. We have a huge open-air worship area which can accommodate a congregation of 300 thousand, but open-air services are fine only in fine weather. What about the pilgrims who come on cold, wet, windy or stormy days? I've watched them so many times, and was deeply sorry for them and for the situation. For many years I've been thinking about building a large church. Thanks to the help of two elderly ladies I managed well-nigh by a miracle to purchase from the Polish State a 9-hectare stretch of woodland which in-cludes the places where Our Lady appeared. I put a perimeter fence round the property and made it ready for open-air services.

It's the world's. largest open-air church, but unfortunately open to all weathers, fine and foul. All the time I prayed for and dreamed of a large church. I bought up from the farmers small strips of land and joined them up into one big estate enclosed by a high monastic wall. I built good approach roads and set up a water supply and drain system, and had an electricity supply connected. I had the designs made. Years passed, until finally the order and permission came from above for the church in honour of Our Lady of Licheń to be built.

AN UNFULFILLED VOW

On 3rd May, 1792, Poland's last monarch, King Stanisław August Poniatowski, the bishops, senators, parliamentary deputies, army, and the entire nation consecrated the foundation stone for the Church of Divine Providence in Warsaw. Then the Partitions came, and the nation was not able to carry out the promise it had made to God. After the restoration of Poland's independence in 1918 work was to resume on the undertaking and funds and materials were accumulated, but progress was so slow that the actual construction work never started. Then war broke out again in 1939, and when it finished an atheist government came to power. Moss and weeds have long since covered the foundation stone that was once laid in Warsaw's botanical garden.

A THANKSGIVING

In 1683 the entire might of the Islamic Ottoman Empire launched an attack against Christian Europe. The Sultan decided to enslave all the European nations and to wipe away the Catholic Church. King John III Sobieski of Poland and Polish forces defeated the Turks and saved Vienna and Europe. After his victory

The Basilica under construction, October 2000

the King sent a message to the Pope, "I came, I saw, and God conquered." To express their gratitude to God for this victory, the Austrians erected a church at Kahlenberg. But I have never heard of any church or chapel which had been built in Poland in thanksgiving for the victory of Poland's forces at Vienna.

In 1920 the onslaught of the Red Army assailed Poland and intended to head west across the whole of Europe. It was stopped on 15th August by a Polish force just outside Warsaw. The event is often referred to as the Miracle on the Vistula. With the help of God the Poles saved their own country and other nations from Communist tyranny. But I have never heard of any special thanksgiving, any votive offering given to God by either the Poles or any other nation in gratitude for this overt miracle.

For 45 years our own nation and the adjacent nations suffered under yoke of Soviet slavery. No prophet dared foretell that that power would crumble under its own weight, that the Red Army would quietly pack its bags, taking away its toys of war, and leave us of its own free will. None other but God Himself endowed our nation with the wisdom and spiritual power which released us from the chains of slavery. Let us keep our eyes wide open; let us give thanks to God with all our power for these marvellous graces. Let us fulfil the promises our fathers made; let us show our generosity before God, just as He has been and is ever generous and merciful to our own generation.

OUR HEART'S DESIRE

On 3rd May, 1991, on the Bicentenary Jubilee of the passing of the Third of May Constitution, on the site of the future basilica at Licheń I erected and consecrated a magnificent, 22-metre larchwood cross. Maybe those vows made by the Polish nation 200 years ago will be fulfilled in the building of Licheń Basilica.

On Saturday, 28th May, 1994, Archbishop Józef Kowalczyk, Apostolic Nuncio, on the Pope's behalf performed the consecration ceremony for the site of the future church at Licheń. On 13th June 1994 Father Jan Rokosz, Provincial of the Marian Fathers in Poland, signed the document allowing the building of the church. On Wednesday, 22nd June, 1994, on the spot where one day the altar holding the Miraculous Image will stand, I blessed the building tools and machinery. I took the first shovelfuls of the digging for the foundations.

On 31st December 1994 the work on the massive foundations for the largest church in Poland (and eleventh biggest in the world) was finished.

On Friday, 26th May (Mother's Day in Poland), 1995, Cardinal Józef Glemp, Primate of Poland, along with many other bishops, archbishops, senior clergymen, priests, and nuns, came to Licheń. A representative of the President of Poland came, too, along with representatives of the regional and local authorities. There was also a huge crowd of pilgrims, venerators of Mary. The authorities of the Marian Congregation, Father General from Rome and Father Provincial and his Council from Warsaw, were present as well. The weather was fine. During the Pontifical Mass that was celebrated the foundation stone of the Basilica walls was laid in a foundation ceremony. The stone had been sent from the Tomb of St. Peter the Apostle, Rome, and it had been personally consecrated by Pope John Paul II. In a marvellous sermon Cardinal Glemb called Licheń a "Bright Meadow" and a "Bright Plain," and said that Our Lady of Licheń was the Patroness of the Good News, the Patroness of the new evangelisation. It was eight o'clock in the evening, and the sun was beginning to set when the ceremonies finished and a splendid procession sct out for the Old Shrine, to visit the church which now houses the Miraculous Image of the Sorrowful Queen of Poland.

Am I dreaming, or is this all really happening? I often ask myself this question. But you have to take God seriously, you can't coax Him with empty words. Although the walls of the new basilica are thick, evidently Mary must have heard my whispered prayers and made use of my work-fatigued, rheumatism — ridden

*C*rowds of pilgrims in front of Licheń Basilica for the consecration ceremony, which Pope John Paul II performed, 7th June, 1999

hands. Man in his smallness, his feebleness, and his powerlessness is faced with the mystery of God's plans, God's Will, God's Mercy and sign for a nation. I am very anxious and afraid, for I am almost alone in entertaining this idea of "the nation's votive offering." There is a lot of red tape to cope with.

On Monday, 26th June, 1995, on the first anniversary of the start of construction and the fortieth of my ordination, in the Rotunda of the Holy Trinity in the Lower Basilica I celebrated a Mass of thanksgiving for all the graces God in His Mercy had bestowed on me during my whole life.

At midday on 29th June 1996 Bishop Bronisław Dembowski, head of the Diocese of Włocławek, consecrated and inaugurated the Golden Chapel of the Most Holy Trinity, which is situated in the lower part of the basilica that is still being built. This Chapel can accommodate a congregation of about 3,000, with 600 seats. It is an exquisitely beautiful edifice. A Pontifical Mass was celebrated, with a superb sermon. Our Lord entered and resides in the tabernacle. Words fail me in describing the deep emotions I felt on that memorable day during the magnificent ceremonies. *Ad maiorem gloriam Dei* — all for the greater glory of God. From that day onwards no pilgrim to Licheń leaves without seeing the Golden Chapel.

WORRIES, ANXIETIES, AND HOPES

The first two years of the construction of this gigantic house of worship are now behind us. I'm on the site every day, not so much to keep an eye on things, as to pray and bestow blessings. I gaze at the design sheets and can't help worrying what will happen next. Will there be enough funds? Will I have enough life and strength? The opinions of those who are sceptical about the whole project. Why such a large church at Licheń? They don't know that we need one as big as this here. In such moments of doubt and anxiety all my support, defence, and hope is in the Blessed Virgin.

I open my heart to Her, I do not keep back the tears and supplications. "O, Blessed Mother, You know all about it..."

"Do not be afraid, My son," She says, "I Myself am building this church in honour of the Divine Majesty and so that My children, from Poland and all over the world, may come to Me. I appoint you My mendicant. Do not be afraid; ask people, stretch out your hands, collect, for there is not much time. I Myself shall find benefactors; I shall touch their hearts with My grace; I shall open up their palms; they shall make their offerings and shall be extremely happy to have contributed their share to such a splendid work. Do not be afraid, My son, none of the benefactors shall become impoverished, for I shall reward each of them a hundred-fold. Look at all that has already been built; I Myself took care of it, so that you should never want whatever was required for it. Trust in God's Providence; trust the people, they love Me and shall not refuse to help in this project."

As I write these words the construction work has been going on for two years and five months. The front Portico of the Arch-angels is nearly complete. So, too, are the two confession naves on the eastern and western sides. The apse and four-storeyed sacristy are only waiting to be roofed. The wall of the 40-metre high chancel is half-built. The columns of the central naves are ascending higher and higher into the sky. You can already see that this church will be not only very big, but also very beautiful: the Polish Nation's votive offering of thanksgiving and supplication to mark the Bimillenary Jubilee of the Birth of Jesus Christ. It's a beautiful and noble idea, although I still can't see that "Nation" involved in the building work! At the moment the entire liability rests fairly and squarely upon the shoulders of the Marian Spiritual Family. People of Poland, dear brethren — please come to my aid!

Dear Friend, I know what strange thoughts are crossing your mind as you read my words. It's like that with Man and his life that we are involved in God's great mysteries, and can never understand it all. I can't understand myself fully, either; I am not fully aware of what's happening to me. I deserve a rest in retirement, a respite in tranquillity before I die, but instead I've been entrusted with a gigantic job to do. Surely my light is near extinguishing. "Do not be afraid, My son," I hear those words all the time in my soul, "you will be My mendicant, and I shall do the building Myself."

Dear Mother of God, You of all people know best how afraid I am and how embarrassed. You know what people will say about me. You know how they treat one who sits in front of a church and begs. One day when I was still a young man a lay brother in the Order took my jacket and wiped the floor with it in Bielany Church. But it was the floor of God's House. What have I to lose today? I might as well be that begging monk, that floor-cloth, so long as the House of God at Licheń is built and glistens with splendour. And if people laugh and mock and ridicule me, if they try to obstruct the job or criticise it, if they turn me away from their doors like an obtrusive beggar, if they throw away my appeals and letters into the litter-basket, or the fire, or the dustbin, why, all the humiliation will be my personal contribution to this church. As a monk I have no money, no gold, no savings. But I have a heart which is full of love for the Blessed Mother of God, for my beloved country and fellow countrymen and women. I donate this lowly offering of humiliation for the building of the church at Licheń.

Perhaps someone will come forward who will be able to augment the glory of the Immaculate Virgin in some way. Maybe there will be someone who will in this way wish to repay Mary a debt of gratitude for Her graces and blessings. Maybe there will be someone who will wish in this way to ask for a long-awaited grace for himself or someone close. Maybe there will be someone who will want in this way to commemorate a dear person's name — a parent's, spouse's or perhaps prematurely deceased child's name in the Book of Founders of Licheń Church. And perhaps this might be the most enduring memorial before the throne of the Mother of God of a son who fell in a war.

Maybe there will be someone who will wish in this way to repay a debt owned to someone no longer alive. Maybe there will be someone who will wish in this way to make amends to God for a sin troubling his conscience. And maybe there will be someone who has had good fortune in married life, or in an examination, in his job, by having good and comely children, in having been able to build a comfortable house for himself or purchased a good car — who will in this way wish to thank God, on Whom all things depend.

I am deeply convinced that the Mother of God will not fail to reward a hundredfold all who contribute — with the grace that they personally need at just the right time.

This Holy Place, and all that is happening here, is the work of the Immaculate Queen Herself, and the work of the hearts that love Her.

It is the work of poor people who have given their widow's mites and generously contributed their labour to the building, decorating, and maintenance. It is the work of boys and girls who have devoted part of their holidays to work in the Shrine.

Licheń is the property and small treasure of the entire Polish Nation, and the Image of Our Lady of Licheń is a sign of our Nation's covenant with Mary, a sign of Mary's love for us. She Herself discovered this Image in a woodland thicket; She Herself said She wanted to be venerated in this Image. That is Her will. No wonder, then, that a heart in which there is Polish blood, cannot pass by this place with indifference. Every Polish man and woman who is a Christian should care about making the honour of the Queen of Poland as glorious and as widespread as possible throughout Poland and the world. The French are proud of Lourdes, and the Portuguese of Fatima. We Poles also have many reasons to feel pride and joy. We give Mary our deepest love in return for Her great love for us.

It is every Muslim's desire to make a pilgrimage to the sacred city of Mecca at least once in his life, and to pray at the place where Mohammed prayed. It is the desire of every Polish heart to make a pilgrimage at least once in its life to the Sorrowful Queen of Poland and to pray before this most Polish of holy images, which Mary Herself discovered and chose as Her own.

***

Dear Brother and Sister, I have related an outline history of Licheń, so that you, too, may learn of Our Sorrowful Mother and may come to love Her deeply, at Her hands receiving the graces and spiritual assistance you need.

After you have finished reading this brochure, do not throw it away. You may have a friend or family member to whom you could pass it on. Give it to them; let them find out about the reasons for Mary's visits in Poland, and what She said and asked for during Her apparitions.

Let people find out about the message from the Sorrowful Queen of Poland; let Her warnings, which are so pertinent today, move our consciences, so that we may avert the wrath of God for our sins, and that we may enjoy His mercy, care, and protection; and peace may reign throughout the world.

Let this little book pass from hand to hand, from home to home; let people read it and anguished hearts be comforted through it; let it strengthen those whose faith is feeble, let it kindle fading love, let it traverse the whole of Poland and the whole of the world, wherever there are people of Polish blood. Let it serve as Mary's supplication and weeping, calling us to mend our ways and to repent; let it be a bell summoning us to save our country and turn our Nation away from the moral abyss and from biological annihilation.

This land, this sky, these waters and this air, these towns and villages, these mountains and hills, this sea, these forests, meadows and lakes, these churches and industrial plants, these people with their kind Slavonic eyes and hearts — this is our family home. The future and the present, the treasures of the spirit and material treasures, the heritage of our culture and learning — they are all part of our native land. No other land in this world is or will ever be ours. This beautiful land in the very heart of Europe was given to us by God many centuries ago. It has been hallowed by the blood of its defenders — knights, soldiers, and martyrs. This land feeds us and is a sacred burial ground, in which the mortal remains of so many generations of our forefathers have been laid to rest, and to which one day we ourselves shall be consigned.

O, Mary, native of the Holy Land, O, Blessed Virgin of Nazareth in Galilee, You called on our land many centuries ago and You have become our very own, You are so Polish and so close. You have placed our emblem on Your bosom and You have assumed our name.

You are not only the Queen, but also the dearest Mother of all the Polish people. Teach us to love God and all that makes up our native land. Renew our souls, protect us, and keep us from hell. We put all our trust in You.

Your Shrine, Licheń, is not a tourist spot. There are no historic monuments here, no magnificent architecture or works of art. Licheń is a holy place, today's Nazareth, the place where the Best of Mothers lives and awaits all Her children. On this hilltop every grain of sand has been a witness to the prayers of generations.

The Shrine of Licheń is a place where the great battle for immortal human souls is on. Mary is gaining the victory. Here the greatest miracles are taking place in human souls: conversions, general confessions, a change in the lives of sinners, momentous reconciliations in families, married couples, friends at war with each other. Here the important decisions in life are taken. Here mothers have prayed for and been granted the grace of a vocation for their children Here many a young person has promised the Mother of God to rise up and go forth to serve Christ in the priesthood. Here Man's reconciliation with God and with his Fellow Man is taking place.

In the fullness of time the entire Polish Nation, from East and West, from North and South, shall come to its Sorrowful Queen, shall pay Her tribute and in this place draw great grace and spiritual power.

There will come a time when alongside the Miraculous Image of Mary, the Cross of Christ, a treasured memorial of the Polish Nation's wartime suffering and riddled with enemy bullets, will receive even more veneration.

WHY ARE WE BUILDING?

There are cogent reasons for hurrying to complete this blessed undertaking for the greater glory of God.

In 2000 we shall be celebrating the 150th Jubilee Anniversary of the Our Lady's apparitions at Licheń. We should give fitting thanks for the gift of these apparitions and for the countless graces bestowed on the Nation through Licheń.

In 2000 we shall be celebrating a grand Jubilee, the Bimillenary of the Birth of Christ, Son of God, on Earth. Licheń Church is to be the Polish Nation's votive offering to God in thanksgiving and supplication.

Times are very hard, insecure, and dangerous for Poland and the world. Prophets of doom are foretelling the imminent end of the world. We have to beg God for mercy, assistance, and rescue. Unless God stretches out His mighty arm over us to pluck us out of our moral and material misery, we shall not manage on our own. We shall be quarrelling and slandering, robbing, hating and destroying each other, just as we did at Babel. We shall become the laughing-stock of the world, an object of contempt, the slaves of the rich.

Let us be united around this noble idea; may the Holy Spirit descend on us once more and transform our thoughts, our lost hearts, our misguided paths.

Millenarian expectations were in the minds of many as the first millennium of Christendom was drawing to a close. Many people were waiting for the end of the world, and numerous sects sprang up. There were innumerable false prophets and visionaries. Our Lady was said to have appeared to many, almost in every village and town. Many abandoned their homes and livelihoods to roam the countryside in quest of these alleged apparitions. Others consumed their entire fortunes on food and drink, since the end of the world was nigh, they said, and therefore it was not worth while saving or doing anything. But there were also others, who put their trust in God and the Church, not in the false visionaries.

In those troubled times, nearly a thousand years ago, Boleslaus the Brave, King of Poland, and the Holy Roman Emperor Otto III, came to Gniezno to the tomb of St. Adalbert (Wojciech), and there before his relics laid the foundations of the Church in Poland, consolidating the beginnings of the Polish State. They left the concern for the end of the world to God, and themselves carried out their duties zealously with all the due care for their peoples and their peace, happiness, and salvation.

In our times, too, there is no lack of sectarians, false prophets, and visionaries. Hardly a year goes by without there being some report of Our Lady, Our Lord, or even all the Saints, appearing somewhere or other. Advice or clarifications from the bishops and clergy on such matters turn out to be of no avail. There is a plethora of beautifully bound books and pamphlets published, containing garbled accounts that have no relation at all with the Church's teaching. Those who have an unfavourable attitude to religion ridicule them on television and in the press, but there is never any shortage of gullible people. As soon as their faith in God fails them, they will believe in nothing at all, or anything and anyone. The end of the world is bound to come, but neither the angels nor even Our Lord Jesus — according to His own words — know the year, date, or exact time when this will happen.

For many people, not only the elderly, "the end of the world" means the end of their own lives or of the lives of their dear ones. Thus they need to hurry, to make amends for the wrongs they have done, the sins they have committed, and to leave something good in this world as a remembrance of themselves.

There is no person who has no pleas to address to God for assistance and blessing. May this church be our personal gift of thanksgiving and supplication to the Divine Majesty. If in spite of these hard times we shall succeed in completing this church and instituting Divine services in it, millions of people will pray for it for many centuries, perhaps even until the end of time. Some of these prayers will be offered for our souls, for our families, for the benefactors. Posterity will call our generation magnanimous, devoutly Christian, and sincerely charitable, if they judge us by the church we built.

A VERY HUMBLE REQUEST

Dear Reader, perhaps as you have been reading this booklet the Blessed Mother has been letting you know that She needs you as well. Perhaps you, too, are being invited by Mary to make an active contribution to this work in Licheń which She has started Herself through people. Dear Friend, I appeal to you as Our Lady's almoner, as Her begging priest, to make a gift towards this church. Offer up to God your prayers, your hard work, your suffering and any annoyances you might be receiving from others, even close persons, for this intention. Offer up your sincere heart, and the information you pass round about this project in the circle of your family and friends. And if you are fortunate enough to have the material means for it, make a donation to our building fund, your own contribution to the bricks and mortar of this church, in token of your gratitude to God for the gift of your life and all the blessings you have enjoyed, in token of your reverence and love for Mary, Who is your Spiritual Mother, too. Maybe today you are healthy, comely, vigorous and wholesome, happy and prosperous, maybe you are doing well and think you don't need any blessings from God. If that's the case, then thank the Lord God for the gifts of health and beauty, talent, prosperity and success. But it often happens that the whole edifice of our good fortune can crumble within a moment. A tragic accident, a serious illness, a wrong done us by others, make us turn to God for rescue, and call on the help of the Blessed Virgin. Or perhaps we might be good fortune's favourites from cradle to grave. But even then the final day will come for us, and our light shall be extinguished. We shall not be taking anything whatsoever of our goods from this world with us into the next. If during our lives we show a concern for the House of God and His Mother, then most certainly Mary will prepare a fine dwelling-place for us in the next world.

Our Beloved Holy Father Pope John Paul II has bestowed his blessing on our building enterprise. We also have the blessing of the Marian Congregation's General, Father Adam Boniecki, from Rome.

We have received the blessing of the Bishop of Włocławek, Bishop Bronisław Dembowski, and his Suffragan Bishops, Czesław Lewandowski and Roman Andrzejewski.

Father Jan Rokosz, Provincial of the Marian Fathers in Poland, and the entire Marian Family, both its community and spiritual members, are very happy that this building scheme is going ahead.

Every day I receive many letters of congratulation, and also from well-wishers who express their satisfaction with the project and hopes that good progress will continue to be made. Donations are also coming in, so up to the present I have been able to cover all the expenditure on a running basis. I am on the building site every day, praying for the people working there and bestowing blessings on their work.

On Sundays and holy days, and also secular holidays when the builders are not at their workplaces on the site, I hold services of thanksgiving on my own. I thank God for the 49 years I have spent in my beloved Marian Congregation; I thank Him for my 41 years in the priesthood; I thank Him for the 31 years of my life I have spent working at Our Lady's Shrine at Licheń. I am grateful to God for the boundless graces I have received, and for the numerous bestowals of spiritual suffering and of physical ailments. I thank Him for the Marian Spiritual Family, and for the group of diocesan and conventual priests I have helped in retrieving their way to the Divine Altar.

I thank God for all the spiritual and material growth that He has granted this beautiful Shrine on Licheń Hill. Finally I give thanks to Our Lord on behalf of all of you as well as myself for letting us initiate the building project for the new church at Licheń.

It is my sincere hope that in a few years' time we shall be able to accomplish this task. Then, at the dawn of the Third Millennium, we shall sing a glorious *Te Deum*. To Our Lady of Licheń, the Sorrowful Queen of Poland, we shall hand over the golden keys to the church which will mark the covenant made by the Polish Nation with God the Almighty and Ever-Living.

Every day during Mass we pray before the Miraculous Image of Our Lady of Licheń for Her blessings and graces for all the benefactors and builders of the new church.

If you would like to make a donation to the Licheń Basilica Building Fund, please send it either directly to.

Father Eugeniusz Makulski
62-563 Licheń k. Konina
Poland

or into the bank account of:

Parafia Rzymsko-Katolicka w Licheniu Starym
62-563 Licheń Stary

at

Wielkopolski Bank Kredytowy S.A.
O/Konin
Bank Account Number: 353005-54263-136-73

We look forward to seeing you at Licheń.

***

Dear Reader,

Now my brief outline of the story of Our Lady's Shrine at Licheń is finished. Perhaps it has satisfied some of your curiosity, but of course words cannot do justice even to Licheń's physical reality, let alone its spiritual riches. To really learn about Licheń you have to come here and spend some time here. Only then will you experience the extraordinary emotions this place offers. Nobody has ever yet regretted coming to Licheń on pilgrimage, and I am sure you, too, will receive a host of blessings for the trouble to come here.

Fraternal greetings to all my readers. May God's blessing be with you always.

Father Eugeniusz Makulski
Cuistodian of the Shrine of Our Lady
62-563 Licheń k. Konina
Poland

USEFUL INFORMATION

Times of Holy Mass and Other Regular Services
— Masses on Sundays and holy days: 7.30 a.m., 9.00 a.m., 10.30 a.m., 12 noon (High Mass), evening Mass 6.00 p.m.,
— Masses on weekdays: 6.30 a.m., 7.30 a.m., 12 noon; evening Masses: 7.00 p.m. (summer), 5.00 p.m. (winter),
— The Blessing of the Sick every Sunday at 1.30 p.m. (after High Mass),
— Confessions heard during all services and on request,
— Guided tours of the church-tower, and of the grounds and memorials in the Shrine on request.

In view of the difficulties involved with packaging, we dispatch parcels containing water from Our Lady's spring only in exceptional circumstances. Photographs, holy pictures, and postcards of the Shrine are available on the premises at Licheń or may be sent by post. A plenary indulgence may be obtained at Licheń all year round, on any and every day of the year. Very many people benefit from this privilege and make a pilgrimage to Licheń at a time which they find most convenient for themselves, individually, with their families or in groups of friends. Many come to make a general confession at Mary's Shrine and to start a new, better life.

The special feast days observed at Licheń are as follows:
— The Feast of St. Dorothy, Patron Saint of Licheń – 6th February,
— Inauguration of the year's festivities in the Woodland Chapel – 1st May,
— The first Sunday in May,
— The first Sunday in June,
— The first Sunday in July (the pilgrimage of the sick),
— The last Sunday in July (the drivers' pilgrimage),

— Sunday before 15th August – inauguration of the ceremonies for the Main Feast,
— 14th and 15th August – Main Feast, anniversary of the apparitions and coronation,
— Sunday after 15th August – Main Feast ceremonies for those working on 15th August,
— Feast of Our Lady of Częstochowa – 26th August (held in the old church),
— Feast of Our Lady of the Rosary – the first Sunday in October.

***

THE MARIAN FATHERS have been working at Licheń since 1949. The Congregation of the Marian Fathers was founded in Poland over 300 years ago, by the Servant of God Father Stanisław Papczyński.

THE MARIAN APOSTOLIC COMMUNITY comprises priests and lay brothers called by God to serve Christ and His Church, under the guidance and following the example of THE LORD'S IMMACULATE HANDMAIDEN in pastoral and educational work in and beyond Poland.

If you or someone you know would like to obtain more information on the Marian Congregation, its history, spirituality, and its current work; and also if you would like to find out about the conditions candidates applying to the Congregation (for ordination or as lay brothers) are expected to meet, please write to the following address:

Księża Marianie
62-563 Licheń k. Konina
Poland

***

Dear Mother of God, Seat of Wisdom, our Sorrowful Queen, I entrust this book to You. I beseech You to bless all those who will read it; visit their homes and bestow graces on them bountifully; protect them from sadness and misfortune; fill their hearts with joyful trust and kindle a love for You in them; bring them into Your Marian Family; and ask God to grant them many blessings on earth and eternal salvation for their souls.

***

PRAYER TO OUR LADY OF LICHEŃ

O, Beloved Mother of God, Mary, Sorrowful Queen of Poland! You are not only the Queen but also the most loving Mother of all the people of Poland Teach us to love God and all that makes up our Country. Renew our souls, protect us and keep us from all evil.

Help us to build this magnificent church on Licheń Hill in honour of the Blessed Trinity and for Your Glory.

O Mother, we place all our trust in You. Amen

CONTENTS